I Thirst
Forty Days with Mother Teresa

Joseph Langford, M.C.

Augustine Institute
Greenwood Village, Colorado

Augustine Institute
6160 S. Syracuse Way
Greenwood Village, CO 80111
Tel: (866) 767-3155
www.augustineinstitute.org

Cover Design: Lisa Marie Patterson

ISBN: 978-1-7327208-8-6

Library of Congress Control Number 2018954334

Printed in Canada

Mother Teresa, Saint Teresa of Calcutta (1910–1997), the founder of the Missionaries of Charity, was a figure known and loved around the world for her work among the poor. Born in Albania, she entered the convent of Loreto at age eighteen and went as a missionary to India a year later. In 1946, on a train ride to Darjeeling, she had a profound encounter with Christ that led her to a new vocation of serving the very poor. She started going into the streets of Calcutta to bring comfort and help to those most in need. In 1950 she received permission to found her new Society. The Constitutions of the Missionaries of Charity spoke of its aim as satiating the thirst of Jesus by serving the poorest of the poor, and in all the chapels of her sisters, Mother Teresa had Jesus' words from the Cross—*I thirst*—inscribed next to the crucifix.

Fr. Joseph Langford (1951–2010) co-founded with Mother Teresa the Missionary of Charity Fathers in 1984 and was the author of *Mother Teresa's Secret Fire* (OSV, 2008). He recognized in Mother Teresa's encounter with the thirst of Jesus and her emphasis on satiating that thirst a powerful symbol of God's love for each person and a road into experiencing that love more profoundly. The meditations gathered here are from the text of his unpublished notes for the retreat on Mother Teresa's spirituality that he regularly gave both to the Missionaries of Charity congregations and to many other groups.

Contents

III. Our Lady's Example

IV. Thirst in the Service of God

V. Sharing in the Thirst of Christ

VI. Jesus, the Incarnation of God's Thirst

VII. Satiated Thirst

Introduction | Mother Teresa and the Thirst of God

In his thirst, the dying Christ seeks a drink quite different from water or vinegar. Now, on the Cross, Jesus thirsts for a new humanity which should arise from his sacrifice in fulfillment of the Scriptures. The thirst of the Cross, on the lips of the dying Christ, is the ultimate expression of the desire of a baptism to be received and of a fire to be kindled on the earth, which had been manifested by him during his life. Now the desire is about to be fulfilled, and with those words Jesus confirms the ardent love with which he desired to receive that supreme "baptism," to open to all of us the fountain of water, which really quenches the thirst and saves.

—Pope St. John Paul II (General Audience, 1988)

Jesus is God, therefore his love, his thirst, is infinite. The aim of our [Missionary of Charity] Society is to quench the infinite thirst of a God made Man.

The first words of our Constitutions, the aim, "I thirst"—are we too busy to think about that? The words, "I thirst"—do they echo in our souls?

I do not know whose thirst is greater, his or mine for him.

—Mother Teresa (1950; Instructions, 1980; Letter, 1980)

Everyone associates Mother Teresa with work among the "poorest of the poor," a mission that she inaugurated among many peoples on every continent. But few have any idea of her real message, of the hidden fire that burned within her and urged her on to do all that she did with such compassion and love.

The message behind all of Mother Teresa's missionary activity is simple but staggering: in the poverty and Cross of Jesus, God has revealed his thirst for us and for our love. Yet this is more than just a verbal message; it is first of all a reality to be encountered and experienced, over and over again, ever more deeply.

When Jesus was suffering on the Cross, one of the cries that came from his lips was "I thirst!"* What does this cry of "I thirst!" express? First and most importantly, it expresses God's thirst for us. Jesus, speaking in his divine nature, revealed something about God that we would otherwise not have known: that God thirsts for us and for our love. But speaking in his human nature, Jesus also revealed something about us that we may never have known: that man is a living thirst for God. The cry "I thirst!" refers to both God and man. Ever since the Fall of our first parents, both God's thirst for humanity and humanity's broken thirst for God has gone unquenched. God had intended there to be a continually quenched communion of thirsts between himself and his human children, but instead there was only distance and separation. On the tree of Calvary, for the first time since the eating from the fateful tree of Eden, the thirst of God and the thirst of man were brought together in complete harmony in the Person of Jesus.

The divine cry "I thirst!" echoes throughout the whole of salvation history. The Old Testament is a careful and magnificent preparation for the full revelation of the Lord's

---

* Jn 19:28.

thirst on the Cross. Jesus had come to fulfill the revelation of God's thirsting love already begun as a distant echo in Adam and Abraham. Jesus brings all these threads of revelation together in himself. Those Old Testament figures prepared his coming, and, in his light, we can see the fullness of their meaning and beauty.

Creation itself is a spilling over of God's infinite thirst to love and to be loved, even beyond the borders of the Trinity. It is the fruit of a divine expansiveness to share this love. The creation of the angels, the bringing forth of the material universe, the creation of man and woman, our own unique creation—all are expressions of God's infinite thirst to love and to be loved.

Think of the thirst that seems inborn in the created universe. Creation ceaselessly thirsts for God the Creator, without whom it cannot exist. Even inanimate creation is a symbol of this universal thirst for God. Yet man is the greatest reflection of God's thirst, since he alone is created in God's image. If God is a thirst, then so too are we: a living thirst to love and to be loved.

Then think of the Fall. God is life, and when our first parents turned their thirst away from him and toward the self, they brought death upon themselves. Both God's thirst for man and man's frustrated thirst for God were immeasurably increased after the Fall.

God then chose Israel as a symbol and channel of his thirst for humanity. He traced out their path to restoration by giving them the great commandment to thirst for him. Love desires, thirsts for intimacy: for the opportunity to know and be known by the beloved, and to share life together.

The covenant bond established between God and Israel was spoken of by God as his marriage with his People. He chose the most complete symbol of mutually thirsting love. The Song of Songs symbolically prefigures the wedding of God and humanity; the final chapters of the Book of Revelation portray its fulfillment with the marriage of the Lamb.

When God's thirst is united with human thirst, as it was on Calvary, miracles of grace and resurrection occur. Here we find the secret to the Christian vocation: the union of these two thirsts in our own hearts. Too often, what is missing in this desired union of thirsts is our own thirst for Jesus. If we look closely at Mother Teresa we will find that her single most striking characteristic—beyond her charity, beyond her zeal—was her profound thirst for Jesus. This then is the doorway through which to walk if we wish to deepen our own experience of the thirst of Jesus for us, the same door that opened God's thirst for Mother Teresa: the renewal and the deepening of our own thirst for him. Our thirst for God is the unseen element that completes the mystery of Jesus' cry of thirst as both God and man on Calvary. Our thirst for God is the same element that allows us to re-create the fullness of that mystery in our own lives. If we wish to experience resurrection power and life, both of these elements need to be present as they were at the Crucifixion: Jesus' thirst for us and our thirst for him.

Jesus desires, thirsts for, our own thirst for him, not as a mere bit of sentimentality, but as an all-consuming impetus of the soul, through which we open ourselves entirely to him in trust and surrender ourselves completely to him in love.

No matter how far I may have traveled in my knowledge and experience of Jesus' thirst, the only path to deepen that encounter is for my own thirst for him to be renewed. What is equally important, my thirst for him is the only way to satiate his thirst. Again, we come up against this amazing truth: Jesus thirsts for my thirst.

This is that dual thirst, of God for humanity and of each of us for God, that Mother Teresa experienced internally, and that she sought to communicate to all whom she met and touched. The purpose of these pages, despite their human poverty, is to encourage and assist you in your own encounter with Jesus' thirst—an encounter that can change your life and the lives of those through whom you touch him every day.

Prologue

Day 1 | The Woman at the Well, Part I

There came a woman of Samaria to draw water. Jesus said to her, "Give me a drink. . . . If you knew the gift of God, and who it is that is saying to you, 'Give me a drink,' you would have asked him and he would have given you living water."

—John 4:7, 10

Our aim is to satiate the infinite thirst of God, not just for a glass of water, but for souls. Souls are immortal, precious to God.

—Mother Teresa (Instructions, 1983)

The dynamics of divine and human thirst can be seen with great clarity in John's Gospel, in the account of Jesus and the Samaritan woman (see Jn 4:1–30). In this encounter, Jesus carries on a lengthy conversation with a woman of Samaria who has come to draw water from the town's well. Through this conversation, Jesus leads the woman from a first experience of his thirst, on toward full conversion and zeal.

Mother Teresa was fond of saying that we are made "to love and to be loved." Everyone thirsts for love. In this gospel encounter there is symbolic importance in many of the details of the meeting. The well of water symbolizes the search for love, the place where people come in their thirst to find relief. Samaria, whose inhabitants were thought by the Jews to be

far from God, symbolizes a life of sinful wandering. Jesus has
arrived at the well and is sitting by it, tired out. We can see that
even before we begin our search for God, even in the midst
of our sins, Jesus is already there waiting for us. He has tired
himself out in his long search for our love.

The Samaritan woman symbolizes our human poverty.
As a Samaritan she had no religious dignity in Jewish eyes,
and as a woman of the time she occupied a subordinate social
position with little power. We can see her as representing the
emptiness, the alienation from God, and the loss of human
dignity that has come about through self-centered thirsts. Yet
she desires love, and, in her search, she has come to draw water
"at the sixth hour" (noon) when the heat, and therefore her
thirst, is greatest. At the very moment of her greatest need, at
the very place of her mistaken human search, Jesus speaks to
her: "Give me a drink..."

The woman is at first reluctant. She replies, "How is it
that you, a Jew, ask a drink of me, a woman of Samaria?"
(v. 9). She is voicing our own hidden doubts and hesitations
before the invitation of the thirst of Jesus: "Can he really mean
me? Does he really thirst for me? Maybe a saint like Mother
Teresa, yes, but me? How could I ever satiate his thirst?"

Jesus shows us that "giving him something to drink" is not
ultimately our gift to him, but rather his gift to us. Only in
the encounter with his thirst can our own desire to love and
be loved be satiated. Jesus' thirst for us awakens our thirst for
him. If we ask, if we thirst for him, he will us give another and
better "water" than any we have found before: the living water
of his infinite love.

"Jesus said to her, 'Every one who drinks of this water
will thirst again, but whoever drinks of the water that I shall

give him will never thirst; the water that I shall give him
will become in him a spring of water welling up to eternal
life'" (vv. 13–14). Again, the meaning is symbolic. The one
who seeks only human love to quench his or her thirst will
be thirsty always, for mere human love, especially when it is
sought selfishly or sinfully, can never satisfy the depths of the
human heart. But those who seek love in God will never lack,
will never be empty, and will never thirst in vain. The more
they thirst, the more Jesus will fill them with his own thirst for
them, which is his love. He does not need exterior means to
communicate that love; it will become a living source within
them, always growing, until finally it will overflow into the
fulfillment of eternal life.

"The woman said to him, 'Sir, give me this water, that I
may not thirst, nor come here to draw'" (v. 15). The tactic has
worked. For the first time the woman expresses her thirst for
what Jesus has promised to give. This is the turning point in
her conversion. She had already met Jesus' thirst for her, but
nothing had changed until she allowed his thirst to awaken her
own. The thirst of God touched the thirst of the woman, and
the miracle of grace began.

The Samaritan woman has taken a crucial step forward.
Not only is she moving toward thirsting for Jesus, but she is
beginning to make that thirst her one desire. She wants a
love that will not need constant replenishment from without.
This is important for her transformation. Conversion means
the gradual passing from a thirst for Jesus *and others* (persons,
possessions, events, and circumstances) to having only *one*
thirst—Jesus. The woman has begun to realize a great truth:
that all other thirsts will not only fail to satisfy her, but those
thirsts tire out her soul. To thirst only humanly drains and

fatigues, even in the midst of ease and success. To thirst for God energizes and enlivens, even when accompanied by toil and trial.

Day 2 | The Woman at the Well, Part II

So the woman left her water jar . . .

—John 4:28

We have been created to love and be loved, and God has become man to make it possible for us to love as he loved us. He makes himself the hungry one, the naked one, the homeless one, the sick one, the one in prison, the lonely one, the unwanted one. . . . He is hungry for our love.

—Mother Teresa (Nobel Peace Prize Acceptance Speech, 1979)

Let us continue our meditation on the meeting of Jesus and the Samaritan woman. After she has requested from Jesus the water that will last, he gives her a seemingly random direction. "Jesus said to her, 'Go, call your husband, and come here'" (Jn 4:16). In saying this, Jesus is not looking for an opportunity to condemn the woman. He is inviting her to take a final step toward satiating both him and herself by examining her false thirsts. At first, she only acknowledges her general state of infidelity and illegitimate thirst: "I have no husband" (v. 17). But Jesus responds by telling her that she has had five husbands. He wants her to discover in detail the existence of all her false thirsts, one by one, for unless they are acknowledged and seen as false, they will continue to oppress her.

Jesus then says to her: "And he whom you now have is not your husband" (v. 18). Here Jesus is showing her that her false thirsts are not just mistakes; they are infidelities in love to the one who alone is the spouse of the soul. By clinging to our various human thirsts—our desires, our limited hopes, our possessions, our plans and ambitions—in a sense we "espouse" them. And in each case Jesus reminds us that this "is not your husband." The thirst you have joined yourself to is not your true spouse. If we persist in such thirsts without any effort to examine them, we wound not only ourselves but the Lord.

"The woman said to him, 'I know the Messiah is coming . . . when he comes, he will show us all things.' Jesus said to her, 'I who speak to you am he'" (vv. 25–26). It is as if the woman had said: "I have heard about and have felt within me the truth of what you say; and maybe someday, when things are better, when life is less complicated, when 'the Messiah comes,' then I'll be able to do something about all this. Later." But Jesus is speaking to her now. The time has come. The Messiah is here. There is no need to wait for a different situation or a better set of conditions. Jesus is present even now to teach us how to satiate his thirst to the full.

Finally, grace triumphs in the woman's heart. She puts down her water jar: she no longer needs her old false thirsts, her previous means of seeking love. She has come to trust Jesus, and, in an act of surrendering her old life with its many thirsts, she goes joyfully to share the invitation of Jesus' thirst with others, an invitation not just to believe, but to experience that thirst for themselves.

The encounter of Jesus with the woman at the well shows us that when Jesus reveals his thirst for us ("Give me to drink"), he is trying to awaken our thirst for him ("Give me this water that I may not thirst"). Once we begin to express our thirst for him, to bring these two thirsts together, our conversion and our satiation begin.

What then is this thirst for Jesus, for God? How is it expressed? It is not simply a feeling, though it may touch our feelings. It is a desire of our will, and therefore it is always possible to us, whether we happen to be experiencing consolation or aridity. Our innate poverty, our weakness, all our needs are already a great thirst. Our interior being is a living thirst that needs only to be directed to God. If this were not so, what hope would any of us have of answering Jesus' invitation? But we have a potent thirst already at work within us. It needs only to be purified, unified, and focused on God in Christ.

Once we have begun to thirst for God, we become aware of many other thirsts that war against that thirst, secret motives and desires that we may not admit to ourselves nor even be fully aware of. Like the Samaritan woman, we need the courage to allow the Lord to point out to us our "five husbands"; we need to let him reveal our many false thirsts so that we might leave our water jars behind us and pursue the one thirst that can satisfy us.

Jesus is thirsting for our thirst. Let us then, like the Samaritan woman, lay aside all those old water jars, and like Mother Teresa, let us fill the well of our hearts with that "one thing necessary"—our profound thirst for Jesus alone.

I.

The Dynamics of Thirst

Day 3 | Rivers of Living Water

**On the last day of the feast, the great day,
Jesus stood up and proclaimed, "If any one thirst,
let him come to me and drink. He who believes in
me, as the Scripture has said, 'Out of his heart shall
flow rivers of living water.'"**

—John 7:37–38

*My children, once you have experienced the thirst,
the love of Jesus for you, you will never need, you will
never thirst for these things which can only lead you away
from Jesus, the true and living Fountain.*

—Mother Teresa (Letter, 1993)

All of God's plan is contained in the verses above from
John's Gospel.

To appreciate their context, let us relive the scene. Jesus
had gone privately to Jerusalem for the Feast of Tabernacles,
one of the three great pilgrim feasts of the Jewish year.
On this joyful feast the Jewish people would celebrate the
bringing in of the harvest in a festival that recalled God's
desire—his thirst—to dwell among his People in a simple tent
("tabernacle" from the Greek) during the forty years in the
desert. To commemorate God's care during those desert years,
the Jews would erect small tabernacles and symbolically live in
them during the feast. God's loving presence at that formative
time of their history was like life-giving and refreshing water
in the dry emptiness of the desert. He was their living water.

The Feast of Tabernacles began with seven days of celebration. On the eighth day, the "great day" as it was called, a magnificent procession was held, led by the high priest. As the procession began, the high priest would take a golden cup and go to the pool of Siloam, a refreshing reservoir of water that represented God's healing and restoring action among his people. The High Priest would fill the cup with water from the pool and hold it up for all to see; he would then lead the people through the city, singing the verse from the prophet Isaiah, "With joy you will draw water from the wells of salvation" (Is 12:3).

The procession would eventually march out beyond the city walls, where the high priest would symbolically pour the water from the pool onto the dry desert ground. This gesture represented not only the renewal of Israel, but the eventual satiating of all the nations' thirst for God by a universal outpouring of the living waters—the Spirit of Love—as foretold by the prophet Ezekiel. Every human heart was one day to become a "tabernacle" for God's living waters.

On this occasion, Jesus is present for the celebration. We can only imagine what is transpiring in his soul as he watches and perhaps participates in the procession. He knows that he is the feast's fulfillment, that he is the one sent by the Father to satiate man's thirst for God and God's thirst for man. He is so deeply moved at the sight that he stands up and cries out in a loud voice: "Come to me all you who thirst!" (Jn 7:37).

This one phrase contains in summary all that God has wanted to say to man from the beginning of time. It expresses God's thirst for man: "Come to me!" It invites man to focus his thirst on God: "All you who thirst." And it promises to fully satiate him with "rivers of living waters" (Jn 7:38). Jesus himself is the golden cup; it is he who pours out the living waters of the Spirit upon the thirsty ground of our souls.

Through the symbolism of the Feast of Tabernacles, Jesus is inviting us to rediscover, in salvation history and in his personal dealings with us, all the various manifestations, foreshadowings, and revelations leading up to the full revelation of his thirst in us and for us. We too can celebrate this feast in spirit. We too have been called into the desert, and Jesus has long been with us, and is even now awakening in us the thirst for living waters.

Day 4 | Sin as False Thirst

I was thirsty and you gave me drink.

—Matthew 25:35

How do we know that God is thirsty? On the cross Jesus said, "I thirst." He was not asking for something to drink. When they offered Him vinegar he didn't drink it. . . . Very often we too offer bitter drink to Jesus. This bitterness comes from the depth of our hearts and wells up in our words. When we give this bitterness to one another, we give it to Jesus.

—Mother Teresa (Instructions, 1977)

If life with God means thirsting truly, then one way to understand the essence of sin is as false or misguided thirst. God made us incomplete in ourselves alone; he created us to depend upon his life and love to sustain us in being. Thirst for that life and love is thus part of how we were fashioned. But our thirst for God can go awry, and we can pursue false paths, seeking and thirsting for things other than God, usually for our own self-exaltation. We need to consider this theme carefully. It is easy to take our false thirsts and their bad effects too lightly.

Our world tends to minimize the destructive nature of sin. We need to remember that sin brought death upon us all. Sin separated us from God. Sin brought Jesus to the horrors of the Crucifixion. Sin would be our complete undoing, but for the mercy of God in Christ.

Sin is the total disruption of God's plan for us. By running after false thirsts, we unravel God's hopes. By rejecting his thirst and giving him vinegar to drink, we pay a great price. We repeatedly risk doing harm to God's plans for us. We need to honestly face the consequences of turning toward false thirsts: the unnecessary pain we have caused God, our families, our friends, the communities in which we live, and those we have been called to serve. As with Mary Magdalene, the depth of our sorrow and repentance will be the depth of our conversion, of our love and sanctity.

Our lack of seriousness about sin is especially present in the way we deal with venial sins, those lesser wrongs that do not immediately destroy the life of God in us. We may be ready enough to avoid the "big ones," but we can become complacent about smaller sins, and this can harm us and lead us on a slow but sure path to lose the life of grace.

It is good to remember the effects upon us of venial sins. They wound the soul, impede the working of grace, deform the image of God, and make the rest of our actions less pleasing to God, since they no longer spring from a pure source, from undivided love. Worse still, they put us on the road to more serious failings. When venial sins remain unchecked, we become ever more distant from God, often without noticing it, until we find that we have wandered far from truth and joy.

The point is not to become a perfectionist; it is rather to avoid the serious spiritual problem of lukewarmness. Lukewarmness, or tepidity of soul, is the state in which we make no authentic effort to escape the patterns of venial sin that we have developed. We should note the telltale signs of lukewarmness. When we find that we have a lax conscience, that we pray only seldom and without much attention, that we are quick to defend ourselves and slow to accuse ourselves, that we have no eagerness for receiving the sacraments, for going to Confession and Mass, that we have made our peace with intemperance in food and drink, that we are content to gossip and criticize others and to hold on to resentments and injuries without seriously trying to forgive—we are in danger of becoming like those Christians from the Church of Laodicea spoken to by Christ: "I know your works: you are neither cold nor hot. Would that you were cold or hot! So, because you are lukewarm, and neither cold nor hot, I will spew you out of my mouth" (Rev 3:15).

Jesus stands at the door and knocks, desiring to live with us. Our first step in overcoming the lukewarmness that can so easily trouble us is to encounter the thirst of Jesus, to experience his unlimited love for us. He desires to set us athirst for him, as he once promised St. Margaret Mary: "I will make tepid souls fervent." This desire in the heart of Jesus should console and strengthen us.

Day 5 | Patterns of Thirsty Attachments

**My people have committed two evils:
they have forsaken me, the fountain of living
waters, and hewed out cisterns for themselves,
broken cisterns, that can hold no water.**

—Jeremiah 2:13

*You need a deep freedom to be like Jesus.
See, he could have been born in a palace, yet
he chose to be poor. . . . Are we so free that we can be
completely naked with Jesus there on the cross?*

—*Mother Teresa (Instructions, 1985)*

Jesus is the perfect manifestation of the Father, the perfect expression of his eternal thirst and plan for us. As we come into deeper contact with the Person of Jesus, the Holy Spirit will show us two things: (1) what God is calling us to, and (2) those areas in which we fall short of his desires for us. It is good for us to note these failings, not so that we can feel bad about ourselves, but to discover important patterns in God's way with us and in our response to him. We wish to see God's strategy for our lives, and we also want to be aware of the contrary strategy of Satan. One way to do this is to uncover our habitual tendencies to certain human thirsts. The devil will be happy to see us overlook these thirsts or justify them to ourselves. The Holy Spirit wants to realign our

19

thirsts with God's plan for us. It can help to consider such attachments so that we can bring them to prayer and set about amending them.

How might we discover our attachments, whether to people or to things, that would cause us undue grief if they were taken from us? Here are some questions we might ask ourselves:

- What is it that constantly worries me? That especially annoys me? That regularly discourages me?

- What makes me angry and moves me to a rebellious attitude to God's ways?

- What causes me to fail in charity toward others?

- What ideas recur repeatedly to me, whether memories, projects, dreams, or desires?

- What thoughts most frequently occupy my mind, in distractions and daydreaming?

As we think through these questions, our attachments will become clearer. What follows are some areas that are commonly vulnerable to misguided thirst, knocking our hearts out of balance.

- A desire to be esteemed, to be seen as successful, to fear failure; a needy dependence on the good opinions of others.

- A desire to be financially well-off, and a tendency to compare ourselves to others and value ourselves and others according to material wealth.

- A desire to be welcomed, to be understood, to be loved, to be praised.

- A desire to always act competently and to have our efficiency appreciated by others.

- A desire to carry out our own plans in our own way; a desire to always be right.

- A desire for safety and security, whether financial, social, or emotional, apart from God himself.

- A desire to impose ourselves on others by vigor, charm, or persuasion.

- A constant curiosity; a desire to be a person "in the know," to be the center of information.

- An attachment to a particular person whose attention we crave and around whom we easily experience jealousy when others gain that person's friendship or esteem.

- An attachment to specific objects, possessions, articles of clothing, favorite foods, or preferred entertainments.

- A desire to organize our time and go through our day according to our sense of comfort.

- An overconcern in matters of physical or emotional health.

Most of these deal with natural and even necessary aspects of human life, and there is a healthy and appropriate way of handling them. But these natural thirsts can easily become diseased, corrupted, or inflamed by the wound in our nature or the whisperings of the devil. The depth of our love and joy will depend on detaching ourselves from thirsts that do not satisfy and saving our hearts for the one thirst for whom we were made.

Day 6 | Jesus the Healer

He went about all Galilee, teaching in their synagogues and preaching the gospel of the kingdom and healing every disease and every infirmity among the people.

—Matthew 4:23

Let us not make a mistake. The hunger of today is for Love. . . . Feeding the hungry, not only for food but also for the Word of God. Giving drink to the thirsty, not only for water, but for peace, truth and justice . . . nursing the sick and the dying, not only of body but also of mind and spirit.

—Mother Teresa (Commentary, 1991)

Jesus leads us ever deeper into life with the Father. As he does so, we receive the outpouring of the Trinity's thirsting love by the gift of the Holy Spirit. This means that we now belong to Jesus, but there remains a big difference between his thirsty condition and ours. His thirst is whole; ours is broken. Our brokenness is itself a thirst. So our healing is the first result of God's gift of "living waters" (Jer 2:13). God wants us to experience his thirst, paradoxically, as a thirst that heals.

In the vision of the heavenly Jerusalem at the end of the Book of Revelation, we are told of the presence of the tree of life, a tree watered by the Holy Spirit, whose leaves are for the "healing of the nations" (Rev 22:2). Healing is Jesus' most important task after taking away the guilt of our sin. This double task of preaching forgiveness and of healing sums up the essence of Jesus' mission.

How does Jesus want to heal us? First, he wants to break the hold of the devil and his lies upon us. Jesus is the one who said to the demon: "Be silent, and come out of him!" (Mk 1:25). Jesus gives us the power to silence the voice of Satan, the deceiver and father of lies. Second, Jesus wants to heal our selfish and broken thirsts through prayer. He heals us of all kinds of sickness, bringing us hope and confidence. He touches each person in a unique way.

Remember the encounter of Jesus with the leper. "When he saw Jesus, he fell on his face and begged him, 'Lord, if you will, you can make me clean.' And he stretched out his hand and touched him, saying, 'I will; be clean.' And immediately the leprosy left him" (Lk 5:12–13). This episode symbolizes the healing of our own spiritual leprosy, the inner corruption that results from our false thirsts. Jesus reaches out to touch the leper, and instead of Jesus "catching" uncleanness from the leper, the leper "catches" purity from Jesus. Too often we lack confidence in the healing power of God, and especially in his desire to heal us. Those words of Jesus—"I will; be clean!"— express the constant heart of Jesus and the Father toward us. Jesus is waiting for us to ask him to heal us, and to listen to those words with faith and confidence.

Remember also the encounter of Jesus and the paralyzed man (see Lk 5:17–25). In that episode, Jesus is teaching, surrounded by a crowd. The sick man's friends or family members bring him forward, and in an act of faith they do their utmost to put him in contact with Jesus. What is the result? Jesus rushes toward him, tells him that his sins are forgiven, and then takes away his paralysis. Having been healed of sin—the greatest healing there can be, for all our misery stems from it—and of sickness, the former paralytic goes home praising

God. As we come to the Lord in confidence and faith, Jesus rushes to us and responds to our faith. He heals the wounds of our sinfulness and our human pain and misery. We then pick up the mat of our misery and walk upright, praising God.

Jesus has two purposes for each of us: he wants to heal each of us by satiating our thirst, and he then wants us to be a channel of his own thirst for the healing of others. But in order to heal others, we must first be healed by opening all our wounds to him. The combination of his love and our brokenness will always bring miracles of healing, in ourselves and in others.

Day 7 | The Need for Faith

**I will pour water on the thirsty land, and streams
on the dry ground; I will pour my Spirit upon your
descendants . . . and they shall spring up like grass
amid waters, like willows by flowing streams.**

—Isaiah 44:3–4

*We also quench the thirst of Jesus by adoration of the
Blessed Sacrament. I see some of you just flop into the
chapel. You are just there, that is all. There is not that zeal
to quench his thirst for you by a personal meeting with him
face to face. Renew your zeal to quench his thirst.*

—Mother Teresa (Instructions, 1977)

We have seen that Jesus is the source of streams of living
water (see Jer 2:13). We might ask, what is it that allows those
living streams to spring up within us? What opens up the well?
The answer is faith, a faith that puts us into contact with the
mystery of Jesus' thirst in all its manifestations. Without faith,
our lives and our service can become a perpetual desert. We
may be working hard, but still we feel empty; we are neither
satiating the Lord nor being satiated by him. Our personal
desert may have its oases now and then, but we rarely make
the effort to stop our rush of thought and our fevered activity
to take the time to drink slowly, deeply, and fully. It is only this
deep exercise of faith that can bring our desert into bloom and
open our empty hearts to the fire of the Holy Spirit. By the act

of faith, our human weakness touches God's limitless power
and infinite love.

If faith is the answer to unlocking the springs of living
water, how can we increase that faith? It will not be mainly
through more learning. It is rather a question of believing
more deeply the things we already know. We may think we
have already grasped the truths of the Faith, when in fact we
are still living on the surface of their truth. It can happen,
though we may not want to admit it even to ourselves, that
many articles of the Faith have little or nothing more to say
to us. We take them for granted; we no longer find wonder
in them or, like Our Lady, ponder them in our hearts. Then
gradually these truths that we "know" begin to lose their
vitality. We still possess them after a fashion. But they have
become fossils—dry remnants of mysteries that were once
living, breathing realities.

As an example, we would all likely give assent to the
statement of overwhelming importance: Jesus died for me.
But what impact does reading or hearing those words have
on us? Do they represent a living truth, something that stirs
our hearts and minds? Do they bring any sense of marvel or
gratitude? And if not, why not? If the great truths of the Faith
are not "good news" for us, how will we witness their goodness
to others?

Why is it, we may ask ourselves, that such momentous
truths touch us so little? Surely it is not that we are entirely
insensitive to the Gospel. It is rather that the foundations of
the Faith have somehow lost their place in our day-to-day
awareness. They have become less real, less present, less a part
of our conscious lives. Deep encounters with the life-giving
mysteries of God then become increasingly rare, and, as our

faith diminishes, the power and fire those mysteries bring to our lives diminish as well.

The only answer to this common problem is a *revival of faith*. We need, not more information about our Faith, but more faith: more faith in our daily contact with the living Christ in prayer, in the Gospel, in the sacraments, in work, in service, in all our daily events. The level of our faith sets the boundaries of our entire spiritual life. It determines not only how much Christ can do through us, but how much he can live in us.

Day 8 | Reviving Our Spiritual Life

**I came to cast fire upon the earth;
and would that it were already kindled!**

—Luke 12:49

*Jesus has a deep and personal longing
to have you for himself. Let him do it.*

—Mother Teresa (Letter, 1973)

Among the greatest dangers to a serious Christian life is a routine of merely superficial contact with Jesus. No amount of shallow contact with the Lord can really change us, nor equal the effect of even one moment of touching him in deep faith.

This means that it is not enough that we receive the Eucharist daily, or reflect on God's Word daily. These are of course excellent practices, and there is nothing lacking on God's part; he continually gives us all we need in abundance. The problem is that our own weak faith can have the effect of quenching the Spirit. Though it is true that the sacraments are sources of infinite power and holiness, we sound their depths only according to the degree of our faith.

The exercise of faith changes us in two ways. First it awakens and intensifies our awareness of Jesus' presence and thirst in our lives. And secondly it increases our readiness to receive him.

Look at the example of the sick woman with a blood flow who approaches Jesus in Luke's Gospel (see Lk 8:42b–48).

The entire crowd is bumping and jostling Jesus. Hundreds of people are touching the infinite source of life, but, interestingly, totally without effect. Then one woman in the crowd touches Jesus, briefly but with deep faith, and she is instantly cured of her illness. Jesus then asks who touched him: not who touched him physically, but who touched him in faith, for he felt the power go out from him.

That same power always emanates from Jesus when he is touched in faith. It is a power that can cure us of years of mediocrity, just as the woman who touched the hem of Jesus' robe was cured of years of infirmity. Jesus wanted her to know, and wanted every generation to know by means of the Gospel, that she had received his healing power not because she was more deserving than others, but simply because she touched him in faith. "Daughter, your faith has made you well; go in peace" (Lk 8:48).

This Gospel provides us with the key to benefiting fully from our daily contacts with the Lord. Simply put, we need to be sure that we are touching him in faith. Why not examine those daily contacts right now? Why not ask ourselves honestly: how much deep faith-contact with Jesus do we experience, whether at Mass, in personal prayer, in reading the Word of God, in bringing our sins to the Lord in Confession, or in going through our day? A deeper and richer faith—not simply an emotion—is within the reach of all of us, for the seeds of that faith were planted within us at our Baptism. We have only to use and exercise this precious gift, and it will surely and steadily grow.

Without this daily contact of deep faith, we each know at what levels of mediocrity and rationalization we can find ourselves. Yet in all our weakness and infidelity we are immensely loved, even thirsted for, by the Lord. His hope in us, and in what his grace can make of us, goes far beyond the barriers of our own discouragement. Can we find the courage to let go of our self-centered concerns and touch the Lord each day in deep faith and surrender?

There is a simple resolution each of us can make that has the potential to radically change our lives. Let us take the trouble always to establish faith-contact with the Lord at key moments of the day. Before we begin our prayer or our work, as we are starting upon an activity or beginning our service, let our minds rest in faith upon the Person of Jesus, and let us remember his presence and his promises. Without faith our prayer is not true prayer, our work is not really done for Christ, and our service is not his service. With faith, all is changed. We will still have our struggles and distractions, but we will be touching the hem of Jesus' robe, however briefly, every day of our lives, and power will go out from him as healing grace comes to us.

II.

Prayer as Thirst

Day 9 | Come and See

**They said to him, "Rabbi" (which means Teacher),
"where are you staying?" He said to them,
"Come and see." They came and saw where he was
staying; and they stayed with him that day.**

—John 1:38–39

*"I have chosen you." Never be tired, Sisters, of repeating
that sentence. We have been chosen for a purpose:
to quench the thirst of Jesus for souls.*

—Mother Teresa (Instructions, 1976)

We can often feel a great loss when we lose the sense of freshness
and intimacy with the Lord that we experienced when he first
called us. We can fall into living simply a "Christian life" as
a general pattern to which we are conforming, and we can
forget the unique and personal love that has called us into
faith. When the Father uttered the Incarnate Word, our own
call, our own "word," was already contained in the mind and
the plan of God. The invitation Jesus gave to the two disciples
to "come and see" is an eternal call, an occasion for our
invitation to come and see the glory of Jesus at the Father's
right hand. God is eternally fresh and alive. It can happen that
we grow stale by force of routine, at which point we need to
enter again the freshness and vivid life of God's call.

The two disciples of John the Baptist—one of them was
Andrew—had been given news of Jesus by another. John had

pointed to Jesus and spoken compellingly about him. John's recommendation was enough to gain their interest, but it was not enough for them to become disciples. They go after Jesus, and then ask him the decisive question: "Where are you staying?" "Where can you be found? What is the shape of your life? What are your interests, your concerns, your habits? We have heard something of you, but we would know your life more intimately."

The reply Jesus gives them is a consolation to every hopeful disciple: "Come and see!" Jesus opens the door wide, saying to them, "My life and my ways are yours to share; my friendship is readily offered; my road of love and truth are more than available to you. Come and see, come and share, come and live with me." Let us remember who it is who is saying this: not just a man, not even just a notable rabbi, but the Lord of the universe and the King of the angels. He speaks these words to every person he has brought into being: "Come and see what you were made for. Come and know the love of the Father. Come and see where I live. Come home!"

Later, these two would become fishers of men and would bring others to Jesus, but that did not happen right away. First, they had to find and to get to know Jesus themselves. "Come and see. I live in my Father and in his will; I live in my word to you; I live in my thirst for you and in my thirst to bring you to the Father." The time will come when Jesus will call these disciples to take up their crosses and walk with him to crucifixion. Their ability to follow him down that path will come from their experience of living with him.

Let us hear these words addressed personally and specifically to each one of us. Whatever roads of service or suffering the Lord may call us to, it will come from his self-gift of love for us and of our love for him. Let us come and see where he lives; let us share his life and experience his thirst for us, and through us his thirst for others.

Day 10 | Elements of Prayer

**If a man loves me, he will keep my word,
and my Father will love him, and we will come to
him and make our home with him.**

—John 14:23

*It is very important for us to know that Jesus is
thirsting for our love, for the love of the whole world. . . .
Ask yourself: have I heard Jesus directly say this word
to me personally? "I thirst. I want your love." . . . If our
hearts are pure, really surrendered to him, this thing
becomes part of our thirst to love him better.*

—Mother Teresa (Instructions, 1983)

If we wish to be true disciples, we must be convinced of the absolute primacy of prayer. But not of just any kind of prayer. It is faith-filled prayer that opens us to the Spirit of Jesus in all his power.

The Apostles watched in wonder as they saw Jesus pray, and they asked him to teach them. We need to have the same wonder and request the same lessons. We need to learn that we have the same relationship of communion with Jesus that he had with the Father, and that by our friendship with Jesus we enter also into his own relationship and communion with the Father.

Prayer is not so much "something" as it is Someone; not so much a method or mechanism we perform (though these may be valid aids) as the springing up of the living waters of the Holy Spirit given us in Baptism. The Holy Spirit is constantly, day and night, praying within us, waiting for us to open to the mystery of his prayer and to enter into it. Even while we pray he is supplying for all our defects. Paul writes, "The Spirit helps us in our weakness, for we do not know how to pray as we ought, but the Spirit himself intercedes for us with sighs too deep for words" (Rom 8:26).

There are three main elements that make up Christian prayer. The first is the task of clearing away the "rubble" within us as preparation for inner solitude and silence. The second involves opening ourselves to the living waters by the act of faith. The third is our response that flows with the living waters in loving surrender. Let us look at each of these three in turn.

To enter prayer, we first need to remove the rubble, to turn from all that is contrary to the Holy Spirit so that the pure spring of living prayer may begin to well up within us, even to the point of becoming a foretaste of eternal life. We all possess the promised fountain of living waters. But most of us have covered up that living spring with layers of debris, such that the Spirit's stream has become only a trickle. We have allowed the voice of the Spirit's prayer to become stifled within us and have admitted many other this-worldly voices to occupy our attention and our hearts. So, we need to clear away whatever is merely human, whatever is not God, in order to create an inner space of silence and solitude free from worry, resentment, impatience, desires, and plans.

The next step is the all-important act of faith that places us in contact with the source of living waters within us— Christ. In that moment our prayer becomes his, and his prayer becomes ours. Remember that the act of faith is not a feeling. It can be a graced help to be touched by feelings of God's presence, but our feelings are not God. Only faith touches God directly and deeply. We need not panic if we feel that "nothing is happening," any more than we would grow concerned at not feeling our blood circulating through our body. We know the blood is circulating, and we go about our business just as securely as when we can feel our heart pumping. We know that the Spirit of Jesus is always at work within us, and we go about our prayer just as securely as when we can feel his presence.

The last element in prayer is to pour ourselves out in harmony with the Spirit in surrender and self-gift. God's thirst, which we meet in prayer, always expresses itself as a gift to us. Similarly, our thirst for him that we express in prayer takes the form of self-gift. This self-gift can be expressed in many ways—as communion, as praise and adoration, as reparation, or as intercession.

We surrender to the Lord in prayer not only our spirits, but every aspect and detail of our lives in all their concreteness. Each time we pray we take our entire existence into our hands and present the whole of it to the Lord—everything inside us and around us, everything that touches us in any way. Our posture before him says: "I and all that I have is yours. I give you the freedom to give me anything or to take away anything you may desire, to change or to rearrange anything in my life. I give myself to you unreservedly and unconditionally. I am yours."

Day 11 | Entering Deep Prayer

Have no anxiety about anything, but in everything by prayer and supplication with thanksgiving let your requests be made known to God. And the peace of God, which passes all understanding, will keep your hearts and your minds in Christ Jesus.

—Philippians 4:6–7

If we only "say" prayers then naturally you may not be praying. To pray means to be completely united to Jesus in such a way as to allow him to pray in us, with us, for us, through us! This cleaving to each other, Jesus and I, is prayer. We are all called to pray like this.

—Mother Teresa (Letter, 1983)

If we plant a seed in the soil of genuine prayer, we will reap the harvest in abundant life. As our prayer is, so shall our lives be. But why is our prayer so often unsatisfying? Why do we hear so much about the power of the Spirit, and yet so often lack spiritual energy? Why do we lose, or never seem to be touched by, the fire Jesus came to bring? Often it is because our prayer has not grown along with the rest of our lives. As our burdens have increased, our prayer has not deepened and kept pace with them, and we find ourselves depleted. The superficial prayer we knew in the past is no longer sufficient to sustain and nourish us today. It cannot fill the deep reaches of our spirit. So our thirst for the Lord goes unquenched. If this state of affairs continues for very long, we can become dissatisfied and discouraged.

The problem is not so much our lack of conversion, for prayer itself will convert us. It is rather our lack of what we might call deep prayer. In prayer, quality is more important than quantity. Superficial prayer that never makes the effort to go deeper cannot satisfy us and cannot satiate the Lord. Instead we need to dive beneath the surface of our souls to find God's presence in what the eastern Church Fathers have sometimes called the "prayer of the heart." At the superficial level we are easily assailed by thoughts and distractions. The living waters are flowing at a deeper level below all the surface disturbances. We are like divers seeking fine pearls. If the diver stays at the water's surface, he is buffeted by wind and waves. When he descends more deeply to where the pearls are to be found, he may be aware of the sea raging above him, but he is not disturbed. So it is with prayer. If we make the effort to stay "deep" at the level of the heart, we may be aware of distractions going on above us, but they do not impede our prayer.

How do we enter deep prayer? Rather than something we simply do, deep prayer is opened to us by faith, through a recognition of the Lord's active presence in the depths of our souls. Then, as we remain with him at the deep level where he dwells, we surrender ourselves to him. It is then that we experience his thirst, and that we satiate him with our own.

There are two phases in this prayer experience: the first is passive, the second active. The first phase is the expression of our thirst to be loved by God. It is one of passive receptivity, as the Spirit prays within us, "Come, Lord Jesus." A novice once came to the great Carmelite mystic St. Mary Magdalen de Pazzi complaining that she did not know how to pray. The saint told her to spend the rest of her prayer that week in the garden, and learn how to pray from the flowers. As the flowers kept their petals ever silently and receptively open toward the sun, in good weather and in bad, constant, unassuming, and secure, so this young novice was to instill in herself a spirit of receptive openness to God's Spirit.

The second phase involves actively sharing in the Spirit's prayer, allowing the Spirit to catch us up in a movement of self-gift. This movement is expressed in praise, adoration, and intercession, as we express our thirst to love God. The Holy Spirit moves within us to declare that Jesus is Lord of our lives and of all we have. He inspires us to say with Jesus, "Abba, Father" (Gal 4:6). We experience not only Jesus' thirst for us, but the Father's thirst for us in Jesus. And finally, we come to enter and share the infinite mutual thirst and satiating love between the Father and the Son in the Holy Spirit, the foreshadowing of eternal life.

What then is required for this deep prayer? It demands two things that are always within our reach: faith and the Holy Spirit. We have no need to wait for ideal conditions, for more time, for greater energy, or for a better emotional state. We need only to begin to pray, and to make use of the many small moments of prayer throughout the day as opportunities of contact with the Lord. Solitude of spirit, generosity of heart, and a sincere desire to know the thirst of Christ will aid us in entering deep prayer.

Day 12 | The Importance of Trust

Even the hairs of your head are all numbered.

—Luke 12:7

Loving trust is only the fruit of total surrender.
You cannot have trust unless you are one with a person.
Total surrender and loving trust are twins.

—Mother Teresa (Instructions, 1983)

Trust is a key element of our spiritual lives. Trust leads to surrender to the will of God, and surrender leads to joy. To know God is to trust him. If we do not know him, we will not trust him.

Without trust, our faith is fruitless and sterile, like Satan's knowledge. Without trust, our charity is paralyzed by fear and resistance. Trust contains an element of both faith and charity, yet it is distinct from both. Trust has its roots in faith; we might say that it is applied faith. Trust is the attitude and act of applying our faith to our lives, today, right now. It involves sharing God's vision of our lives and seeing ourselves with his eyes. Trust perceives God in events and sees events in the light of God. The foundation of trust is faith in God's real, present, and active involvement in all things, no matter how small. Trust means believing that "in everything God works for good with those who love him" (Rom 8:28), not just in general terms, but especially in this present matter that I am facing. Trust means taking our eyes from the immediate event and lifting them to God, its proper context and source. Trust is an opening to God, allowing him to incarnate himself in our personal history.

Jesus was constantly trying to instill in those to whom he preached an unshakable, childlike trust in the Father.

Trust is a conviction that we lack nothing, within us or outside of us, and that all is going forward according to the plan of the Father. Trust sees the hand of the Father everywhere, as Jesus did, even as he went to his Passion. In that supreme trial, Jesus did not need to wrestle anew with each specific event because he saw, in the events unfolding before him, the hand of the Father, even to the point of dealing with Judas and with Pilate. Trust is a vision that penetrates the veil, the "distressing disguise" that often conceals the face of God in others. Trust is an attitude of mind and heart that allows God to be the true Lord of our lives.

There are two aspects to this attitude of trust: one is general, the other is concrete and specific. The general attitude is often called confidence. Our lack of confidence in God pains him, sometimes more than our sins. He necessarily comes to us shrouded in the events that make up his loving providence, and he longs to see us receiving him in those events, not pulling away from them when they disguise his presence. Confidence in God means a readiness to see the seeds of resurrection even in the midst of suffering and darkness. But to be of real value, this general attitude of confidence in God needs to be applied specifically and concretely in our present situation. We want to gain a habitual response of trust to all the events of our lives. We want to respond to whatever happens with the conviction that this too is within the plan of our loving Father, who has numbered the very hairs of our heads, and who delights in giving us the very best.

Day 13 | Growing in Trust

**Behold, I am the handmaid of the Lord;
let it be to me according to your word.**

—Luke 1:38

*My own Jesus, do with me as you wish, as long as
you wish, without a single glance at my feelings and pain.
I am your own.... I want to satiate your thirst with every
single drop of blood that you can find in me.*

—Mother Teresa (Letter, 1959)

If trust in God is so important for our spiritual lives, how can we deepen our trust? Many of our problems with trust come because we don't understand the object of our trust. The object of trust is not the confidence that God will give, or do, or change, whatever we are asking of him. It is rather confidence in our union with him, the firm belief that whatever is happening now is the best that could happen to advance that union.

We regularly need to confront enemies of trust. One of these is a "surface" or superficial vision of our lives, when we take things at their face value and fail to see their deeper meaning. This is an easy mistake to make, but it does great damage to our life of faith. While genuine trust leads to stability, equanimity, and serenity both in sorrow and in joy, a superficial view of things leaves us tossed about by the waves of whatever is happening to us.

This surface vision can then lead to superficial hopes. Rather than hoping in God and all that he wills, we can pin our hopes and desires on superficial things. Instead of hoping for God's presence and the fullness of what he has planned, we find ourselves only hoping for this or that immediate event or thing. This brings in its train anxiety, distraction, and discouragement, since such false hopes always ultimately fail us. Even our most "holy" desires can be enemies of trust, if they are founded on self-will, self-reliance, or self-generated vision. Real trust can blossom only in an atmosphere of docility and dependence on God.

Trust is of especial value when we find ourselves in the midst of one of life's storms. Again, the object of our trust is not the absence of any storms. God does not promise to save us *from* the storms, but he does promise to save us *in* the storms. He rescues us and brings us through the tempests, and he uses them for our good. Trust is not a pious game; it is an eminently practical habit of relationship. To trust in God is to live in reality, free from illusions. Part of the reality of trust means recognizing that we are only limited and impoverished creatures, absolutely dependent on God. It requires humility to accept our limitations and our powerlessness in the face of God's plans. Trust is therefore an aspect of poverty of spirit: the readiness not to need to know why, not to demand, not to set conditions, but instead to choose and embrace what God has planned or allowed for our good.

To be genuine, trust must be unconditional. It only works when it is whole and entire. Just as water is always wet or it is not real water, so trust is always unconditional or it is not real trust. There is no such thing as occasional trust. It is no exaggeration to say that the fundamental decision we will make is whether or not we will give to God genuine—one hundred percent—trust. Everything else depends on this one decision, this one attitude, because God can only work in us if we trust him.

Our Lady trusted God completely, and her act of trust allowed the Word to become incarnate within her. In an analogous way, the fruit of our trust will be the "incarnation" of the Word, God's own thirst taking flesh in our lives. The more our trust resembles that of Our Lady, the more fully will we bring about this incarnation so longed for by the Lord. This is why there is so much power in making her response our own: "Behold, I am the handmaid of the Lord; let it be to me according to your word" (Lk 1:38).

Day 14 | The Eucharist

**Jesus said to them, "I am the bread of life;
he who comes to me shall not hunger; and he who
believes in me shall never thirst."**

—John 6:35

*See the humility of God. He made himself the hungry one
to satisfy our hunger for God through our love. . . . See the
unity between prayer and wholehearted free service. We
meet Jesus in the Bread of Life in the Eucharist and the
humanity of Christ in the distressing disguise of the poor.
We must be able to unite both of these. . . . Prayer by itself—
No! Work by itself— No! These two have to go together.*

—Mother Teresa (Instructions, 1978)

In the light of the divine thirst, what is the meaning of the
Eucharist? Thirst always expresses itself in gift, and gift in turn
reveals thirst. God has so thirsted for us as to become one with
us, to give us his Body and Blood in order that we may become
transformed into him. The Eucharist is the sacrament of the
thirst of God—the sacrament of that supreme moment on the
Cross—a thundering echo of "I thirst." It is the total gift of
God's thirst to satisfy our thirst for him and for his love.

Like the Apostle John who first heard the cry of thirst
from Christ, we too are there at the Cross, thanks to the gift
of the Eucharist. What does it really mean to be present at the
Cross? On Calvary Jesus' words are addressed to the whole
world: "I thirst!" In the Eucharist, they are addressed to each

of us. The living echo of "I thirst" is being spoken to us in all its fullness. The Eucharist is the supreme gift that contains all other gifts. In the Eucharist, God our Father is making a total personal gift of his Son to each one of us. All that Jesus is and all that he has done is poured into our poverty. The power of Christ's thirst in the gift of the Eucharist gives us the power to make our thirst become a gift in return.

This means that everything human in us needs to be transformed and made divine. By the Eucharist we become what Jesus is and we are enabled to do what he has done because he has sent us his Spirit, the fruit of the Resurrection. At the Eucharist a weaving of lives takes place: we enter the Paschal Mystery of Jesus, and he enters and lives in us. By the Eucharist the power of Christ's love enters every moment of time, all of history, and penetrates the world through us, allowing him to continue his praise of the Father and service to others through our lives.

So the gift of the Eucharist to us is not just for us. We are to become a living extension of Christ. His life is to "take flesh" in us. Just as the lowly elements of bread and wine contain the magnitude of God's love, so too the humble conditions of our lives can become a liturgy of praise, adoration, and service. If we ask: where today is Jesus' smile, his words, his hands, his compassion, his voice, his face? The answer is: he lives in our charity.

We are the mouthpiece of the thirst of Jesus and the Father. That is the dignity of our Christian vocation. The power of his Cross present in the Eucharist gives us the power to carry our crosses. The greatest expression of his love leads us to the greatest expression of our love. The whole of our lives is a living continuation of the Eucharist—not ours, but his. Beneath the poverty and misery that can be seen by human eyes, the Father sees the life of his Son. In the Eucharist we become what we celebrate.

This means that our lives must be in harmony with the Eucharist. We, too, shall be broken for others and poured out, but it is Christ who is broken and poured out in us. We become the bread of mercy and intercession for others. We who have received healing become vehicles of healing.

The Eucharist is the bright center of our Faith, the very core of our Christian life.

III.

Our Lady's Example

Day 15 | Our Lady at Cana

**On the third day there was a marriage at
Cana in Galilee, and the mother of Jesus was there;
Jesus also was invited to the marriage, with his
disciples. When the wine failed, the mother of Jesus
said to him, "They have no wine."**

—John 2:1–3

*Be only all for Jesus through Mary.
This is the best way to satiate his thirst.*

—Mother Teresa (Letter, 1990)

Cana and Calvary were the alpha and omega of Jesus' public ministry, the beginning and the end of his work of revelation of the Father's thirst. They are also the two places specially marked by Our Lady's presence.

The mystery of Our Lady's role in the revelation of God's thirst had begun already at the time of her Immaculate Conception. By that gift of grace, Mary became the perfect mirror and vessel of the Trinity's thirst. Then at the angel Gabriel's announcement, she experienced how much God thirsted to love us and to receive our love. For the nine months during which she carried the eternal Word within her, she came to know as no other human creature the depth of God's thirst to be with us. In giving birth to Jesus, she brought God's thirst into the world, and from that day forward, her constant prayer was a pleading with the Father to share with the whole world the living thirst within her. It was God's thirst that pierced Mary's heart according to the prophecy of Simeon.

Now at the wedding feast of Cana, Our Lady opens the floodgates, the "new wine," of Jesus' thirst. On this occasion, when the wine runs out, Our Lady is asking Jesus for much more than refreshment for a celebration. She is pleading with him to reveal himself fully in all his love and in all his thirst for humanity's love. She knew the meaning of the biblical imagery of the marriage covenant between God and Israel, and the wedding at Cana must have seemed to her the perfect setting for the revelation of the depth and reality of the love contained in that image, a love that was fulfilled in her Son and his infinite thirst. She is led to ask Jesus to do at Cana what the prophets had often done in major moments of revelation: to speak God's word and at the same time to act it out in symbol. The changing of water into wine would mean a symbolic change from the water of the Old Covenant to the wine of the Gospel and the New Covenant.

Jesus understands her and what her request means; he sees her desire that he reveal the fullness of his being to the world. He responds that his "hour" has not yet come, meaning by this the offering of himself at the Crucifixion. Mary could not know that the Father had reserved the full revelation of his glory to another "wedding feast," that of Calvary, the real wedding of God and humanity, the true revelation and satiation of God's thirst and man's. Cana was but the symbol of that culminating act, the sign of what was coming.

In the light of the true extent of Mary's request, can we understand Jesus' answer and solve the apparent contradiction between his response and the working of his first miracle. After first seeming to put Mary off, Jesus does indeed respond to her plea, and he does change the water into wine. Yet this was not the hour of fulfillment, but of foreshadowing. That full revelation, the "best wine," would indeed be saved for last, for the time of the Crucifixion at Calvary. Jesus knows that he will answer Mary's prayer fully on the Cross and that she will be present to witness it.

Day 16 | Our Lady at Calvary

Standing by the cross of Jesus were his mother, and his mother's sister, Mary the wife of Clopas, and Mary Magdalene.

—John 19:25

So you see in what way you too can take your stand at the foot of the Cross with Mary, our Mother, and satiate the thirst of Jesus. Let us offer everything to Jesus—every sorrow, humiliation, discomfort.

—Mother Teresa

In the Passion narrative of John's Gospel, we are presented with a striking relationship between Our Lady and the thirst of God. Jesus has been brought to Golgotha and there crucified; and seeing his mother standing near the Cross next to his disciple John, he says to his mother, "Woman, behold your son!" (Jn 19:26). He then says to John, "Behold your mother!"(Jn 19:27).

The Church has understood this act from the Cross to be Jesus' gift of Mary to the Church as its mother. Then immediately after the giving of this gift comes the cry of Jesus: "I thirst!"(Jn 19:28).

From his place on the Cross, Jesus makes an important connection between the gift of Our Lady as Mother and the gift of his thirst. He proclaims the Trinity's thirst for mankind only after providing us with "the Woman" who would care for and nourish that thirst within us. She would protect it by crushing the head of the serpent. The first Eve had led humanity to reject God's thirst; the New Eve was to bring humanity to accept it. These two gifts are forever connected and interdependent. The early Church understood the connection from the start. The first disciples returned to the Cenacle after the Ascension and gathered around Our Lady in prayer. As she had prepared the Church for the revelation of God's thirst on Calvary, so she would prepare Christ's disciples, both then and now, for the communication of that thirst in the outpouring of the Holy Spirit on Pentecost.

Let us return to the scene at Calvary: Our Lady had followed Jesus closely in sorrow and prayer along the Way of the Cross. Now she is at the place of crucifixion, ahead of everyone else. She looks for the disciples of Jesus, his picked men. Will none of them witness the completion of Jesus' mission? Will none be present to see the true glory of God as he is raised up to call all men to himself? Finally, John arrives. He had at first run away like the others, but he overcomes his weakness and makes his way back to Our Lady through the jeering crowd along the Via Dolorosa. In Mary he found a love, a strength, and a serenity that surpassed and sustained his own. He found a heart that would open his own heart, and that would enable him to hear those important words spoken by Christ from his suffering throne. John, the Lord's disciple, was thus brought to encounter and experience the thirst of Jesus through the presence and care of Our Lady. It is a service that she willingly performs for every disciple.

On Calvary, opening her soul to Jesus' cry of thirst, Mary became the woman foretold in Genesis, the New Eve, "mother of all the living." She nurtured the thirst of her Son in John and the first disciples, protecting, purifying, and sustaining it.

Day 17 | Our Lady in the Church

A great sign appeared in heaven, a woman clothed with the sun, with the moon under her feet, and on her head a crown of twelve stars; she was with child and she cried out in her pangs of birth, in anguish for delivery.

—Revelation 12:1–2

How much we need Mary to teach us what it means to satiate God's thirsting love for us which Jesus came to reveal to us. She did it so beautifully. Mary allowed God to take possession of her life by her purity, her humility, and her faithful love. Let us seek to grow, under the guidance of our Heavenly Mother, in these three important interior attitudes of the soul that delight the heart of God and enable him to unite himself to us.

—Mother Teresa (Letter, 1992)

Our Lady's intercession and preparation for the gift of God's thirst has continued well beyond Calvary. It was she who shared with John her understanding of the words they had both heard on Calvary, who communicated to him the fire and urgency those words had impressed on her soul, and who urged him to write them down for the Church. The presence of Our Lady, who had taken John into her heart and whom John had taken into his home at Ephesus, was a constant reminder of the words of Jesus. To hear Jesus say, "Behold, your mother" (Jn 19:27), is to hear Mary say, "Behold his thirst."

After her Assumption into Heaven, Mary's role of intercession was magnified and empowered immeasurably. Jesus had ascended to the Father's right hand, and Our Lady joined him there. At his Ascension, Jesus was given "all power and authority in heaven and on earth." Upon her coronation as Queen Mother, Our Lady received a share in his power and authority—not to be served, but to serve the mystery of Jesus' thirst in the Church and the world.

Wherever the world begins to drift yet again from her Son, there Mary has been found. When the new wine that had begun to flow at Cana is about to "run out" in men's hearts, Mary pleads for us once again, reminding her Son that "they have no wine" for the wedding. Again and again he has answered her plea and responded with grace to her intercession for us.

In our weakness and our wandering, in this urgent "hour" of rejection of Christ all about us, let us imitate John on that day of the Crucifixion and go in search of Our Lady. She will strengthen our hearts and bring us faithfully to our own unique Calvaries, where we will come close to Jesus in the glory of his Passion, and we will hear and touch his thirst. She will bring us close to his Passion in the Eucharist, close to his Passion in our families and our communities, in the poor, and in the poverty of our own hearts, and she will allow our souls to be "pierced," as hers was, by the sword of God's thirst. She will bring us close to the foot of the Cross so that we can satiate Christ's thirst, and tell of his thirst to a thirsting world. But we cannot give to others what we have not first experienced. With Our Lady's help, we, like John, can come to know and can bring to others that "which we have heard, which we have seen with our eyes, which we have looked upon and touched with our hands" (1 Jn 1:1)—the mystery of Jesus' thirst for us.

It has been Our Lady's role and special dignity to bring together the thirst of God and man, as she did first in her womb, as she did at the wedding at Cana, as she did for John on Calvary, as she did for the disciples at Pentecost, and as she will do for each of us in our daily living of those same mysteries. She is the "garden enclosed," the new Eden, the wedding place of God and man in Jesus.

Day 18 | Two Lives, One Vocation

The cry of Jesus on the Cross sounded continually in my heart:
"I thirst!"

—St. Thérèse of Lisieux (Story of a Soul)*

The thirst of Jesus on the Cross is not imagination.
It was a word: "I thirst." Let us hear Him saying it to me
and saying it to you. . . . It is really a gift of God.

If you listen with your heart, you will hear, you will
understand. . . . Until you know deep inside that Jesus thirsts
for you, you can't begin to know who He wants to be for you.
Or who He wants you to be for Him.

—Mother Teresa (from *A Novena to Blessed Teresa of Calcutta*)†

Jesus' original call to the Twelve Apostles to follow him and belong to him stands as the perennial pattern for every vocation, the model for all those who are called to follow Jesus in a special way. Yet the call to love and service is not something generic. Each call within the Church has a specific nature. Each call renders a particular service to the Body of Christ and does so in a unique spirit. What was the special vocation that God had in mind for Mother Teresa? What was

---

* Clarke, John, O.C.D. *Story of a Soul—The Autobiography of St. Thérèse of Lisieux.* Translated from the original manuscripts by John Clarke, O.C.D. Third Edition. Washington, D.C.: ICS Publications, 1996, 99.
† "Jesus Is My All in All," A Novena to Blessed Teresa of Calcutta, edited by Fr. Brian Kolodiejchuk, M.C., Mother Teresa Center. Printed by the Knights of Columbus, 2005, 15.

to be the unique spirit that would characterize her response to his call to love and to serve?

We gain a clue to the answer from Mother Teresa herself, who always understood her own vocation as being patterned after that of her patroness, St. Thérèse of Lisieux. Mother Teresa always had a profound admiration for St. Thérèse's little way—doing small things with great love. Yet the little way, both for Mother Teresa and for St. Thérèse, was the fruit of something else; it was the expression of deep and hidden roots, without which the little way would only be something nice, but not important enough to be an essential part of their vocation.

The origin of Mother Teresa's vocation is well-known: it was an encounter with grace on a train ride to Darjeeling in India on her way to a retreat, where she experienced Jesus thirsting for her love and calling her to satiate that thirst in those who echoed it most, the poorest of the poor. All that she later did and accomplished was rooted in that experience. Why else would she have left her convent of Loreto and gone into the slums, except that she had been deeply touched by the conviction of Jesus' daily thirst for her love and taken by the desire to satiate him where he thirsted most?

What about Thérèse? What were the origins of her vocation and the roots of the well-known spirituality of the "little way"? Could it have been the same as Mother Teresa's? Was there a common experience of Jesus' thirst? At first glance it would seem that there was no obvious common experience of this kind. Yet the connection is there, as a more penetrating look will make clear. In her autobiography, St. Thérèse speaks not once, but eleven times, of Jesus' thirst. And she speaks of his thirst in the same language used by Mother Teresa, describing it as a "thirst for love and for souls."

Not only does St. Thérèse speak of her personal experience of Jesus' thirst, but she places that experience at a crucial point in the story of her life. The initial experience, which stayed with her to the end, occurred on a Sunday as she gazed on an image of the crucified Christ. Years later she would write that the cry of Jesus' thirst had penetrated her soul at that moment, and that the words "I thirst" had "set aflame in [her] a lively and unknown ardor" of love. "I wanted to satiate my Beloved," she writes, "and I felt myself devoured by his same thirst for souls."* She later continues: "I seemed to hear Jesus saying to me as to the Samaritan: 'Give Me to drink'; and the more I gave him to drink the more the thirst of my soul grew."† She called the experience of Jesus' thirst the most precious gift and channel of his love.

---

*   Ibid, 98–99.
†   Ibid, 100–101.

Day 19 | The Little Way and the Thirst of God

(Jesus) has no need of our works but only of our love, for the same God who declares he has no need to tell us when he is hungry did not fear to beg for a little water from the Samaritan woman. He was thirsty. But when he said: "Give me to drink," it was the love of his poor creature the Creator of the universe was seeking. He was thirsty for love.

—St. Thérèse of Lisieux (Story of a Soul)[*]

We are contemplatives in the heart of the world because we have to satiate God's thirst. Whatever we are, whatever we do, it is not what we do or how much we do, but how much love we put into it. How much love! That stupid little thing! Yes, how much love.

—Mother Teresa (Instructions, 1992)

Why is the little way, the practice of doing small things with great love, of such importance to Thérèse of Lisieux and to Mother Teresa? The answer is that the little way is the logical and necessary expression of the vocation to quench the thirst of God for love. In one of her most famous lines, Thérèse joyfully declared: "My vocation is love!…In the heart of the Church, my Mother, I shall be love."[†] Apart from the experience of Jesus' thirst, Thérèse's strong expression of the vocation to love, even to

---

[*] Ibid, 188–189.
[†] Manuscript B.

the point of *being* love in the Church, loses much of its clarity and force. But understood as an expression of the thirst of Jesus for love, Thérèse's vocation to share in and communicate that love becomes both intelligible and powerful.

Because Mother Teresa and St. Thérèse shared a common experience of Jesus' thirst, they also shared a common vocation in responding to that thirst. If the heart of Jesus' thirst was a thirst for love, then love needed to be their vocation.

With the practice of performing little things with great love, the call to satiate the thirst of Christ is always within reach. As a contemplative Thérèse lived the little way of love within the confines of the cloister. Mother Teresa and the Society she founded lived the little way not only by satiating Jesus through prayer, but also by serving his thirst among the poor. Seen in this context, humble works of love become beautiful as the sign and the witness of the love and thirst of Christ.

In the call to love given to Thérèse and Mother Teresa, we can get a glimpse of what God is doing in our time. Never has the vocation to love been more urgent or important than it is now. In his loving plan, God gave the grace of the experience of his thirst to St. Thérèse, who was to live it hiddenly, as Jesus had lived in Nazareth. Just as Jesus' hidden life was a preparation for his public ministry, so too the inner and hidden communication of this grace to the Church through the Little Flower was to prepare the public and visible expression of the same charism and vocation in the very public person of Mother Teresa.

The original pattern of the call to St. Thérèse, retraced in the soul of Mother Teresa, is a perpetual grace to the Church, not only as a pattern for the Carmelites and the Missionaries of Charity, but as an inspiration for all who desire to satiate the thirst of Jesus for souls. Let us then ask St. Thérèse to intercede for us, as she so evidently did for Mother Teresa, that we might be penetrated through by the mystery of Jesus' thirst for love, and that for us as for her Jesus' cry of thirst may resound constantly in our hearts.

Day 20 | The Immaculate Heart of Mary

The angel said to her, "Do not be afraid, Mary, for you have found favor with God."

—Luke 1:30

You can never be "only all for Jesus," if your love for Our Lady is not a living reality. Come so close to Our Lady that she can take you to Jesus. . . . Cling to Our Lady! "Mary, Mother of Jesus, take away all sin from my life." That is satiating the thirst of Jesus.

—Mother Teresa (Instructions, 1982, 1983)

Mother Teresa often insisted that it was not so much a particular work, but rather a particular spirit in which that work was done, that constituted her vocation and that of her sisters; not so much what was exterior, but what was interior. Mother Teresa had a special love for the Immaculate Heart of Mary as pointing to the essence of her call and made the Feast of the Immaculate Heart the patronal feast of her Society. We can see why this might be so. Many of Our Lady's feasts refer to specific events in her life or roles that she plays; but the Immaculate Heart celebrates Mary's interior posture of love. Her heart symbolizes her constant satiating of God's thirst for love. The components of Mother Teresa's vocation—the experience of Jesus' thirst, the vocation to love, and the little

way of humble works—find their first and deepest source in
the Immaculate Heart of Mary.

Our Lady's Immaculate Heart is a model for the whole
Church, for all who have been called to represent and witness
the thirsting love of Christ. Our Lady's trust, her surrender
to the plans of God, her cheerful joy as a gift to others, her
poverty of spirit, her humility, and her thoughtfulness provide
us with a witness of love to learn from and imitate.

But Our Lady is not a distant model who can only be
imitated from afar. She is first of all a presence in our lives,
even as she was for John, a person we can have confidence in,
and recourse to, in all our needs. Mary is present to intercede
for us for a greater understanding of her Son's thirst; she is
present to share with us her own experience of his thirst; she is
present to protect us in our wanderings and to lead us back to
fidelity and generosity. She will bring us to stand with her *juxta
crucem*, "by the Cross" of Jesus' Passion in the world. There at
the foot of the Cross she continues her vigil and mission until
the end of time, and there the Lord continues to declare, for
those who have ears to hear, "I thirst!"

In the Father's plan, all the disciples of Jesus were called
to love God and to preach the Gospel, thereby satiating his
thirst for their love and for souls. But to John was given the
particular mission to be the witness of Jesus' thirst within the
early Church. To be able to fulfill this call, it was essential
that he first come face to face with the mystery of God's thirst
at Calvary. And for that encounter it was necessary that he
cling to Our Lady, both in his discovery of Jesus' thirst on the
Cross, and in his witnessing to that thirst in his later writing
and preaching in Ephesus.

As we respond to the call to satiate God's thirst for man and man's thirst for God, it is necessary that we first come face to face every day with the mystery of Jesus' thirst for us. And as it did for John, this happens as we stay by Our Lady's side. Neither Cana nor Calvary would have been the same for the disciples had Our Lady not been there. Our own personal Cana and Calvary, those times when we encounter the covenantal love of Jesus and empty ourselves with him for the sake of others, will not be all they are intended to be in the Father's plan if Our Lady is not present.

Let us, then, like John, take Our Lady into our homes, into our hearts. Let us stand with her at the foot of the Cross, live with her at Ephesus, and allow her to communicate to us the thirst of Jesus and the way to express and satiate that thirst. Let us recall once more that she, as model of the Church, is the wedding place between God and man. It is she who prepares the wedding (Cana), assists at the celebration (Calvary), and nourishes the guests (Ephesus), bringing about the communion between the thirst of God and the thirst of humanity.

IV.
Thirst in the Service of God

Day 21 | The Secrets of the Kingdom

**To you it has been given to know the secrets
of the kingdom of heaven.**

—Matthew 13:11

*Don't be afraid to be small. Numbers are not what
make the difference, but—are we really his? Our vows
make us big, because we are dealing with God. And
satiating the thirst of God is something big.*

—Mother Teresa (Instructions, 1985)

Christ came to establish a kingdom—the Kingdom of
Heaven. Once we have experienced conversion through our
encounter with God's merciful thirst, we are moved, just as
Paul was moved on the road to Damascus, to ask: "What shall
I do, Lord?" (Acts 22:10). The Father answers that question by
placing us before Jesus and saying: "This is my beloved Son,
with whom I am well pleased; listen to him" (Mt 17:5).

The Father wants to instill in us the desire to give ourselves
totally to Jesus and to respond generously to his overwhelming
thirst. Jesus is the vehicle, the expression, and the channel of
our thirst for the Father and his thirst for us. Responding to
the Father's thirst in Christ leads to satiating his eternal thirst
for us.

The nucleus of Jesus' message and mission is the
proclaiming and inaugurating of this kingdom in favor of

the "poor." All facets of human poverty are the object of the compassion of the kingdom, but the poor to whom the Good News is especially addressed are those who present themselves before God in recognition of their need, their emptiness, their sinfulness, and their thirst. The poor are those who come before him with empty hands in full acceptance of their spiritual poverty. The first condition for receiving the benefits of the kingdom is that of receiving it as a child (see Mt 18:3), humbly yet joyfully recognizing and accepting our need for the living waters. Those who attempt to enter the kingdom through their own self-sufficiency or self-made holiness will be, in the words of Our Lady, "cast down from their thrones" and "sent away empty."

There seem to be four essential principles, four "secrets of the kingdom," inherent in the Good News announced by Jesus—principles that should inform the way we offer service to Christ.

The first of these is *total gift*. The Good News is a proclamation of God's free and unmerited gifts. All of creation and all of revelation proclaim God's freely given love toward his creatures, rooted in the mystery of endless self-gift among the Persons of the Trinity. As Paul reminds us, "What have you that you did not receive?" (1 Cor 4:7). Free gift is the moving force behind the outpouring of God's mercy and the underlying theme of the Good News, the master key to understanding the Kingdom of God. When we accept the free love and mercy of God, we are not made smaller; we grow larger. It is the only path to our truest dignity and freedom.

The second principle is *total trust*. "Do not be anxious about your life, what you shall eat or what you shall drink, nor about your body, what you shall put on.... But seek first his kingdom and his righteousness, and all these things shall be yours as well" (Mt 6:25, 33). Our doubts, our lack of trust, testify against us that we have not fully understood the Gospel. But once we do understand, then we not only proclaim our trust in the kingdom, but we live a pattern of trust. Total trust is a sign that we are in harmony with the kingdom. It sets us free to give the kingdom away.

The third is *total love*. The gift we have received is not to remain fruitless, bottled up within ourselves; it must overflow to others. "You received without pay; give without pay" (Mt 10:8). Friendship with Jesus in the kingdom means that we fulfill the new commandment to love one another. Just as Jesus is loved by the Father and loves us in turn, so we are to continue the same expanding cycle, allowing the Son in the Spirit to love through us. As the Son has loved us, so we have loved others.

The fourth is *total conversion*. Our response to the Good News of the kingdom involves accepting Jesus' invitation to radical conversion. We need to be ready to change whatever needs changing, to do whatever it takes to live as true members of Christ's kingdom of love.

When we have understood the Lord's thirst, we then desire to satiate his thirst and to give ourselves entirely to him—to thirst for him with all of our being.

Day 22 | The Burning Bush

When the LORD saw that he turned aside to see, God called to him out of the bush, "Moses, Moses!" And he said, "Here am I." Then he said, "Do not come near; put off your shoes from your feet, for the place on which you are standing is holy ground."

—Exodus 3:4–6

We are meant to satiate the thirst of Jesus, and this thirst was revealed to us from the Cross. We cannot know or satiate the thirst of Jesus if we do not know, love, and live the Cross of Jesus. We must be united with Jesus in our suffering, with our hearts full of love for the Father and love for souls as his was.

—Mother Teresa (Letter, 1996)

The Book of Exodus tells the story of Moses encountering God in the wilderness (see Ex 3:1–8). At the time of this occurrence, Moses was a refugee, living in exile and looking after the flocks of his father-in-law. At a certain point he sees a bush, blazing with fire, but not being consumed. He turns aside to get a closer look at this strange sight, when God speaks to him from out of the bush. This encounter is the beginning of God's action to free the Israelites from slavery. We can understand it also as an image of the way the Lord comes to each of us.

Notice that it is the Lord who takes the initiative in appearing to Moses. God thirsted for Moses and sought him out, even in the far reaches of the desert. Moses was minding his own business, full of his own thoughts and cares, and God broke in upon him. In the same way, God desires to come into the "burning bush" of our hearts and reveal himself to us, upon his own initiative, and by his free choice.

When God succeeds in getting Moses' attention, Moses begins to walk toward the burning bush; but before he gets very far, God stops him and calls him by name: "Moses, Moses!" (v. 4). The Lord wants to make clear to Moses that this encounter is the fruit of his call; it is his plan and needs to proceed according to his direction. Moses began with simple curiosity, but now he is stopped in his tracks. Touched by grace, Moses then responds, "Here am I." Now Moses' attitude has changed. It is no longer he who is asking the questions; he knows himself to be in the presence of God, and he puts himself in readiness to respond.

As he did with Moses, so God will do with us: he will stop us amid our plans and spiritual pursuits and call us by name. To approach God only from the standpoint of our own plans, worries, and curiosities is to put things backwards. The Lord wants a genuine personal encounter with us, not with our problems and our programs. We are to be an empty canvas before him, in all our poverty, our nakedness, and our nothingness. His thirst for us comes first; only then can we respond with our own thirst for him in return.

The Lord then says to him, "Do not come near; put off your shoes from your feet, for the place on which you are standing is holy ground" (v. 6). The Lord loves Moses and plans to do great things through him. But his love and his plans can only come to fruition if Moses first readies himself and changes his attitude. He needs to put off his sandals, a symbol of a person free to go where he will, and to recognize that he is on holy ground, that he has entered a zone of God's intense presence where reverence and obedience are the only appropriate responses. This is always the way when God comes to us. The first thing Jesus said to the human race was "I love you, and I thirst for your presence." These words were "spoken" by the deed of the Incarnation, by God seeking us out and coming to live among us. The next thing out of the mouth of Jesus was "Repent!" a word that means "Change!" Because the Lord loves us so much, he wants our union with him to be full, and this can only happen if we are ready to allow him to make us holy as he is holy. Genuine love always desires this kind of change in the beloved.

When Moses responds to God's presence and call by removing his shoes and hiding his face, acts of reverence and obedience, God then spontaneously reveals himself: "I am the God of your father, the God of Abraham, the God of Isaac, and the God of Jacob" (v. 6). He then promises Moses that he has seen the affliction of his people, and that he is going to deliver them from all their sufferings and bring them into a land flowing with milk and honey (see vv. 8–9). Moses had not expected any of this; but God's plans were far beyond his own hopes.

So with us: the Lord is aware of, and moved by, our weaknesses and our sufferings. He wants not only to solve our problems and heal us, but to give us more and much greater gifts than we had asked or imagined. He will rescue us, if we do not insist on imposing our own terms and plans. We must let go of whatever we are tightly holding on to, whatever is holding us enslaved, and leave God free to do what he wants, as he wants. If we keep Moses' attitude, we shall receive Moses' gift. And the Lord will bring us into a land of goodness and

life, one that has been prepared for us before the foundation
of the world.

Day 23 | God's Thirst Everywhere Present

For I am sure that neither death, nor life, nor angels, nor principalities, nor things present, nor things to come, nor powers, nor height, nor depth, nor anything else in all creation, will be able to separate us from the love of God in Christ Jesus our Lord.

—Romans 8:38–39

This "I thirst," and "I quench" should make our life fruitful. In every trial, difficulty, misunderstanding, remember these words. . . . The poor are not only in slums but right here in this house. Right here we satiate his thirst.

—Mother Teresa (Instructions, 1984)

If we take seriously Paul's claim that all things work together for the good of those who love God, this means that everything present in our lives is a reflection of God's thirst for us. Nothing is excepted, all is in his hands, and all is his gift. As we continue to consider the thirst of God manifested in our lives, it can be of use to look at three main categories where that thirst makes itself known.

The first of these is the natural world. When we see all the moral and spiritual beauty around us, faith will allow us to see the Lord who is the author of all this beauty, the one reflected in the mirror of his creation. This beauty is the beckoning call of his thirst. It should lead us not to the desire of possession, but to the lifting of our hearts in praise.

The second category of the thirst of Jesus is to be found in the distressing disguise of the wounded, in the harrowing experience of rejected love. However it may have been that human rejection has come upon us, hiding behind that rejection we will find Jesus, thirsting for our generous love and leading us to pray on behalf of those who have wounded us. The same is true wherever we find suffering and woundedness in others around us. That wound is Jesus thirsting in another for our understanding love and consolation.

A third expression of God's thirst comes in the form of obstacles to our union with God. These difficult moments, whether of temptation or distraction, are meant to become stepping stones for us. Just as Jesus ignored the temptations of the devil in the desert and turned his ears away from the jeers of the crowd on Calvary, so he is asking us to share with him those moments of suffering.

These expressions of God's thirst are not mere reflections of God and his love; the Lord in all of his immensity is actually present in all these events. Though this presence is something universal, it always is personal at the same time. We can pray the prayer, "Come, Lord Jesus," in the profound confidence that God is always answering it, in all the details of his creation and in all the events and circumstances that come upon us.

God, who is present in all these gifts, is not present in them passively. He is acting, moving, communicating his thirst for us. We will want to call this truth to mind often until it becomes a habitual spiritual attitude. We will want to train our eyes in faith, such that we can see that in everything around us, the voice of the one who is seeking us is saying: "Come to me."

Day 24 | Charity and the Presence of God

For the love of Christ urges us on, because we are convinced that one has died for all; therefore all have died.

—2 Corinthians 5:14

These desires to satiate the longing of Our Lord for souls of the poor, for pure victims of his love, [go] on increasing with every Mass and Holy Communion. All my prayers and the whole day, in a word, are full of this desire.

—Mother Teresa (Letter, 1947)

Charity is a sign of the kingdom, of the God who revealed himself in word and deed as love. We communicate Christ and we reveal him by radiating what he is—charity—in what we are and do, in words and works of charity. Charity is a true revelation, an incarnation of the Gospel in action. Is Christianity truly the answer to the world's thirst, or are we to wait for another? After once silently observing incarnate love in action in the Home for the Dying in Calcutta, an Indian mullah said to Mother Teresa: "All my life I have known that Jesus was a prophet. But today I know that He is God . . . for only a God could give that kind of joy in serving one's fellow man."

Radical and joyous charity is perhaps the single most cogent proof of God's existence in our materialistic and confused world in which reasoned arguments alone are no longer capable of touching or changing minds and hearts. St. Thomas Aquinas made famous the "five ways" of demonstrating God's existence. But those five ways no longer suffice by themselves for a world starving from its wealth as much as from its poverty. There needs to be a "sixth way," the way of charity—an irrefutable argument, a demonstration, a vision, an experience, through acts of charity, of the Eternal God who is Charity. This "sixth way" is the first way, God's own preferred way of revealing himself "because he first loved us" (1 Jn 4:19).

In addition to revealing God and his love, charity also communicates that love. It not only speaks of God, but in a certain sense it mediates God's presence. Works of charity are works of God, not only because they become his instruments, but because they are privileged with a special presence of the God who is charity.

Charity not only convinces and communicates, it also attracts, taking on a beauty and desirability that speaks both to believer and agnostic, becoming a reflection of the splendor of God himself and a mirror of his beauty. Works of charity are indeed something beautiful for God, for charity shares in God and in his own beauty. In a sense, charity is beauty.

Because it is beautiful, because it attracts, charity elicits a response in kind on the part of the recipient. It invites, encourages, and stimulates; it becomes contagious. Ideals attract only when they are lived. Beauty finds its power only when it is given a form. As Mother Teresa often said, "To learn charity, we need to see it lived." Charity radiates itself and is fruitful and self-propagating with the very freshness and vitality of God himself.

Only those who have received charity can believe in charity. Only those who have seen charity can believe in a God of charity whom they cannot see. But once perceived, this charity leads not only to belief but back again to charity, a newfound charity, which in turn reinitiates the same cycle of belief, attraction, and response in others.

This is our Christian vocation, to reveal God. How is that done? We radiate Christ and proclaim his presence in words and works of charity that, however small, mirror the beauty of the Trinity.

Day 25 | Compassion, the Continuing Thirst of Christ

Jesus went about all the cities and villages, teaching in their synagogues and preaching the gospel of the kingdom, and healing every disease and every infirmity. When he saw the crowds, he had compassion for them, because they were harassed and helpless, like sheep without a shepherd.

—Matthew 9:35–36

One of the most beautiful gifts of God to our community is to serve and to put our love for Jesus in living action in serving the poorest of the poor . . . in giving tender love and care to the poor, to the dying, to the crippled, to the unwanted, to the unloved, to the lepers, and so bring new life and new joy into their lives.

—Mother Teresa (Address, 1992)

We are face to face with a great mystery, begun with the Incarnation and fulfilled on Calvary—the mystery of a God who, in Jesus, so thirsted for man as to take on all our sin, all our poverty and our abandonment, our suffering, our slavery, and our death. All the abyss of misery symbolized in our human hunger and thirst he took upon himself to the point that our thirst found voice in his. God had so united himself to us that Jesus' cry from the Cross was both the Father's thirst and our thirst. When our first parents ate of the tree of Eden,

God's love for man became thirst; on the tree of Calvary that thirst became com–passion, "suffering with," thirsting not only for, but with, a thirsting humanity.

The beautiful and unfathomable reality is that God's compassion continues; Jesus still thirsts with fallen humanity. He not only feels our thirst, but he thirsts in our thirst because he has made us one with him by making himself one with us. Mother Teresa once said, "God has made himself the hungry one, the lonely one, the needy one." Jesus remains our Emmanuel in the poor and in the suffering. It is precisely in our poverty, in those places and times where we feel most the need for God and his seeming absence, that he mysteriously dwells among us. He has become so small, so near to us, so one with us that he hides in our very thirst. There he thirsts with us and for us, and there under the distressing disguise of the poor and suffering around us, he continues to ask, "Give me to drink" from the Jacob's well of our hearts. If in these moments we only knew who it is that is asking us to drink, if we only knew the gift of God, how readily would we respond in compassion to those around us. In seeing the poverty of those around us, we see the poverty of Jesus. When he shows himself in the distressing disguise of the poor, we have also seen the Father, and have discovered the Father's love and thirst. Jesus, present in the poor and the suffering, reveals the thirst of the Father.

How much would change for us if we only took Jesus at his word: "I was hungry . . . I was thirsty . . . a stranger . . . sick . . . in prison . . . [and] you did it to me" (Mt 25:35–36, 40). How many poor and suffering are around us? How many are there in our own neighborhoods? Do we ever find them and share their crucifixion with them?

Compassion for those who suffer is the cornerstone of Christian ministry, first because it is Jesus himself who suffers in the suffering, and second because compassion for physical poverty and suffering expresses, makes authentic, increases, and completes our compassion for the deeper but less obvious spiritual poverty and suffering. Like Jesus, we are called to serve the whole person, to respect the sacramental nature of man whereby spiritual realities are expressed and communicated through outward gestures. We are called to possess and proclaim a deep compassion for man's inner poverty: outer compassion is an integral part and necessary expression of a yet deeper inner compassion.

Through the exercise of compassion, we begin to embrace the distressing disguise of those who suffer, and we learn to love the "unlovable." It is that very unlovableness that is the most crushing of crosses. Mother Teresa would say, "Be kind, very kind to the suffering and poor. We little realize what they go through ... treat them as temples of God." By being treated as "temples of God," those who suffer begin to rediscover their human dignity; our charity reveals the Christ in them both to themselves and to the world.

Day 26 | Staying the Course of Compassion

Let us not grow weary in well-doing, for in due season we shall reap, if we do not lose heart.

—Galatians 6:9

Zealous young professed, the sound of your footsteps in search for souls must be like a sweet music for Jesus. Keep the thirst for souls ever burning in your hearts, for only then will we be true Missionaries of Charity.

—Mother Teresa (Instructions, 1966)

It is comparatively easy to experience compassion and to respond to those who suffer—for a little while. But to stay the course, to love the "unlovable" over time, to walk the extra mile, requires the grace of generosity. Just as Jesus loved us "unto death" (Phil 2:8), we need to learn to love without measure, without counting the cost, to love until it hurts and beyond.

The inevitable fatigue, whether of body or of spirit, that comes upon those who serve others in compassion, is not merely its undesirable by-product; it is an integral part of our service, since our service is grafted onto the redemptive work of Christ. Not only in reaching out to the poor and suffering, but especially in the very fatigue, frustration, and pain it brings upon us, we are sharing in the salvific action of Christ.

The tireless effort that gives substance to our compassion leads us not only to respond to those who invite us into their lives, but also to seek out those who do not, expressing a mercy that not only forgives but elicits conversion.

Like all charity, our compassion, if it is to be genuine, must begin at home, within our own families and communities, toward those with whom we live, work, and serve. It is there that our compassion and our solidarity should find their deepest roots and potential.

Before the immensity of the needs around us and the impossibility of fully meeting them, we must never doubt the value of the little we can do. Rather we are to be always ready to give the Lord our "five loaves and two fish" (Lk 9:13), confident that he will bless and multiply what we bring him according to his will. It is only God's love acting through us that can satiate the thirsting Jesus. Our trust is in God himself, in the power of his Word spoken with our voice, in the small things that leave room for God and his activity.

To love the suffering around us means to be ready to pour ourselves out for them, not merely for the masses, for humanity as a whole, but for each immortal soul, for this person in front of us at this moment. As true with the Eucharist, so also with the poor and suffering, Jesus is equally present in one as in many. Perhaps the best way of showing that nothing is too much for our compassionate love is, paradoxically, to show that nothing is too little, that we are ready to do small things for the few with great love. By this means we can follow Jesus in rejecting the temptations in the desert that we also feel, temptations to seek immediate results and to enjoy hollow praise for our efforts rather than to choose the Father's path of poverty, humility, and patient trust.

Each person we meet is a temple of God. As Mother Teresa always insisted: "Jesus would have died even for one."

Every person's dignity is worth a great sacrifice, for each person is Jesus.

V.

Sharing in the
Thirst of Christ

Day 27 | Peter and the Cross

**Whoever would save his life will lose it,
and whoever loses his life for my sake will find it.**

—Matthew 16:25

*How to approach the thirst of Jesus? Only one secret: the closer
you come to Jesus, the better you will know his thirst.*

—Mother Teresa (Letter, 1993)

An important lesson for the disciples once took place when
Jesus was on the road with his disciples, some months before his
death (see Mt 16:13–28). There had been growing opposition
and hostility to Jesus and his ministry, and he was concerned
to strengthen the disciples' faith and to prepare them for the
coming conflict.

Jesus first asks the disciples, "Who do men say that the Son
of man is?" (v. 13). The disciples answer that people think he
is a prophet like many of the prophets of old. Then Jesus asks
them the important question: "But who do you say that I am?"
(v. 15). He is not looking for just a "catechism" answer here.
He wants to know what he means to his disciples, they who
have come to know him. Enlightened by faith, Peter answers,
"You are the Christ, the Son of the living God" (v. 16). Jesus
then tells Peter two things. The first is Peter's genuine identity:
"I tell you, you are Peter, and on this rock I will build my
Church" (v. 18). When Peter sees who Jesus is, he then is given
the light to see himself. Our identity is so tied to our Creator

and Savior that we can only begin to understand ourselves when we begin to understand Christ.

The second revelation given to Peter and the disciples has to do with coming events. It is only when they have begun to see Jesus truly and to understand that he is not only "the way, and the truth, and the life" (Jn 14:6) in a general sense, but that he has become for each of them their way to the Father, their truth and life, that Jesus reveals the mystery of his coming Crucifixion and Resurrection. Yet, when Peter hears this, he retreats from faith and falls back on evaluating things from a merely human perspective. He finds it difficult to receive the news that the Christ would suffer in this way. Jesus sharply rebukes him: "You are a hindrance to me; for you are not on the side of God, but of men" (Mt 16:23). These were hard words for Peter to hear, to be told that he was hindering his Master. Peter loved Jesus, but his love was still too simply human. He had plans to serve Jesus, but his plans also were too human.

Jesus then follows this rebuke with a general principle: that the way into the kingdom can come only through crucifixion. "If any man would come after me, let him deny himself and take up his cross and follow me" (v. 24). The acceptance of the mystery of the Cross is ever the touchstone of reality. Discernment of our service to Christ and the proper shape of our lives needs to conform to the logic of the Cross, or we will be lost in illusion.

It is important that we embrace this teaching of Jesus with joy, as leading to all good things. We need to make peace with our crosses so that we can carry them, and not just drag them along behind us. We need to become friends with the crosses God sends our way. Jesus revealed the Crucifixion to his disciples and friends just when they grew to a deeper understanding of who he was in the intimacy of love. In the same way he brings us to understand the Cross as we draw close to him in love. The Cross is the most decisive means Jesus uses to express his thirst for us, and it is the most beneficial way for us to live our thirst for him.

Day 28 | Our Wounds as Thirst

Blessed be the God and Father of our Lord Jesus Christ, the Father of mercies and God of all comfort, who comforts us in all our affliction, so that we may be able to comfort those who are in any affliction, with the comfort with which we ourselves are comforted by God. For as we share abundantly in Christ's sufferings, so through Christ we share abundantly in comfort too.

—2 Corinthians 1:3–5

Until you can hear Jesus in the silence of your own heart, you will not be able to hear him saying "I thirst" in the hearts of the poor. . . . Not only that he loves you, even more— he longs for you. He misses you when you don't come close. He thirsts for you, even when you don't feel worthy.

—Mother Teresa (Letter, 1993)

We have been looking at the great truth that God thirsts for us profoundly in Christ and that he wishes to spark within us a profound thirst for him. Here we will want to bring that truth home to us. If we are to rightly embrace this truth, we need to discover the many manifestations of Jesus' thirst in our lives, past and present.

Each of our lives has presented us with gifts that express God's personal thirst for us, hidden yet precious gifts that need to be discovered and rediscovered. It can be a good practice to review our lives through this lens to see the various expressions of God's thirst given to us along the way, whether of personality, of providence, or of the sacraments.

But it is not only in obvious blessings that we can see God thirsting for us. Even our sufferings and our hurts are gifts to us, expressions of God's thirst. How can that be? There is an invitation in whatever we have suffered to love Christ as he has loved us: to bear a part of the Cross that was placed on him by others. Because the Lord loves us, he wants to share his glory with us, and the road to Calvary is the only path to glory. Christ also longs to share with us his greatest joy—that of showering graces upon souls—and we can share this most fully as our sufferings are united to his.

So let us make peace with all of our wounds and sufferings. They are essential to the revelation of God's thirst, and they help us to become more totally dependent on him. The Lord draws us to himself with two hands—with joy and pain. Seen in the light of faith, both joys and sorrows are gifts from God. And because the Cross was the place where Jesus most plainly thirsted for us, our sharing of that Cross will always be the greatest and surest place of meeting the thirst of Jesus. Every detail of every cross has its place in God's plan. As the light of God's thirsting love shines on our crosses, we can see them as God sees them, as his way of drawing us ever deeper into his heart. The Cross seemed to be the greatest moment of darkness, but in reality it was the greatest moment of light, bringing peace, joy, and triumph.

We may be able, dimly, to see how our wounds or sufferings can unite us to Christ; but what about our sins and infidelities? Can they possibly fit in with the plan of God? Can they also somehow be channels of his thirst? The answer is yes, easily so. Remember that God has seen our sins and failures from all eternity, and has already taken them into account, weaving them into his plan for us. Recall the comforting words Joseph spoke to his brothers who had sold him into slavery in Egypt: "Do not be distressed, or angry with yourselves, because you sold me here; for God sent me before you to preserve life" (Gn 45:5). God receives our brokenness, and like a master craftsman he cannot resist restoring us, making us into something even more beautiful than before. As the Prodigal Son discovered, the gift of God's forgiveness and mercy is the greatest expression of his thirsting love for us.

Because of our forgiven sins, the glory of God's thirst for us will shine all the more resplendently for all eternity. We may feel we have marred his plan, but, if we accept his forgiveness, the result will be just the opposite. The thirst of God will be more truly revealed in the merciful forgiveness we have received than our own perfect righteousness could have been.

Day 29 | Poverty and the Thirst of Christ

**Blessed are the poor in spirit,
for theirs is the kingdom of heaven.**

—Matthew 5:3

*If you want to become holy, become poor. Jesus became
poor to save us, and if we really want to become poor, like
Christ, then we have to be really poor, spiritually poor.*

—*Mother Teresa*[*]

It is a noteworthy truth that when God came among us, he chose to come as a poor man. The first expression of God's chosen poverty was the self-emptying of the eternal Word in the mystery of the Incarnation. Love led God to empty himself. The poverty of Jesus was not a value in itself; it was an expression of the Father's love. "You know the grace of Our Lord Jesus Christ, that though he was rich, yet for your sake he became poor, so that by his poverty you might become rich" (2 Cor 8:9). Chosen poverty is above all charity, so charity inevitably leads to the desire, even the need, for poverty. As Mother Teresa often said, "Love and poverty go together, hand in hand."

Paradoxically, when we choose poverty, the involuntary poverty of our human condition finds its only true wealth as it

---

[*]   Mother Teresa. *Where There Is Love, There Is God*. Edited by Fr. Brian Kolodiejchuk, M.C. (New York: Doubleday, 2010), 238.

is enriched by God. To love as Jesus loved, we need to desire
a certain poverty because chosen poverty is basic to the inner
dynamics of love. Love leads by nature to the desire to share
what one has with the beloved, and sharing means that we
empty ourselves by giving what is ours to others, and that we
take on their needs and sufferings.

Love also leads naturally to the desire to serve, and service
requires that we undergo an inner emptying that will allow us
the freedom to serve. Though primarily an inner disposition,
genuine poverty also needs outer expressions. Jesus made
himself poor to be able to love. If we wish to love we must
likewise willingly make ourselves poor, whether this is in
embracing a consecrated life of poverty, or in giving as we are
able of our time and resources to those in need.

Jesus did not have to become poor; it was not pressed upon
him. He consciously chose poverty for his mission. Consider
how constant was the outer manifestation of his inner poverty:
he was born in a stable; he spent thirty years as a humble
laborer; during his public ministry he had nowhere to lay his
head; he was then taken as a prisoner and nailed to the Cross
as a criminal, thirsting, betrayed, and abandoned; he was
finally laid to rest in a borrowed tomb. If Jesus chose to be
poor in order to express his love and accomplish his mission,
is it not clear that we who are to be a sign of Christ, another
Christ, also need to choose poverty? Achieving the degree of
poverty the Lord asks involves a gradual process of inner and
outer self-emptying.

Interiorly we will need to live the humility of Jesus,
in detaching ourselves from ambition and the desire for
possessions, in seeking the lowest places, in habitually putting
aside our false thirsts for temporal riches of whatever kind.

Exteriorly, we will need gradually to simplify our lives, to find ways of incarnating our spirit of inner poverty, to choose not to own or use certain luxuries. Exterior poverty expresses and reinforces our "yes" to God.

The Cross was the culmination of the self-emptying of Jesus, the most complete consequence of the Incarnation and the supreme revelation of our thirst for God and God's thirst to satiate us. The Cross was not an isolated or accidental event; it was the triumphant expression of Jesus' inward and outward poverty, his double crucifixion of spirit and flesh. The Cross is a living out of poverty, and poverty is a living out of the Cross.

The fruit of such poverty is joy. Let us not go away from Christ sad, like the rich young man, but instead be filled with the joy of union as we remain, in the poverty of love, with the one who satisfies our deepest thirst.

Day 30 | Suffering with Christ

Beloved, do not be surprised at the fiery ordeal which comes upon you to prove you, as though something strange were happening to you. But rejoice in so far as you share Christ's sufferings, that you may also rejoice and be glad when his glory is revealed.

—1 Peter 4:12–13

How Our Lord must love you to give you so much a part in his suffering. You are the happy one, for you are his chosen one. Be brave and cheerful and offer much for me that I may bring many souls to God. Once you come in touch with souls, the thirst grows daily.

—Mother Teresa (Letter, 1952)

Our call to follow and satiate the Lord is not just a question of serving him, but even more importantly of suffering with him. For this we need an interior disposition of self-gift. Jesus invites us to suffer together with him, to take part in the work of redemption, not only in our hearts, but in our spirits and flesh as he did. To share the mystery of the redemption necessarily means to suffer. Jesus did not save the world by his preaching, but by his suffering and death. Jesus accomplished the Father's plan precisely in his suffering, in choosing to embrace the details of the Passion that the Father had preordained, in all of their horror and injustice, for in this suffering the glory of the Trinity's thirsting love shone forth.

Peter tells us not to be surprised by suffering. It is the Father's plan for our glory, to satiate us fully in his Son, and to give us the happy chance, and the eternal honor, of having satiated his Son in return.

By the help of the Holy Spirit, we can come to a place of personal commitment to share in Jesus' sufferings, to allow him to continue his mission of praise, salvation, and satiation concretely in our daily lives. This is the reason for our coming into this world: to share in Jesus' "hour" and to satiate, proclaim, and channel his thirst to the world, just as he did—from the Cross.

Suffering is our work; it is our mission. Our wounds are the wounds of Jesus, who continues his glorious Passion within us. Because he lives in us, we have a share in his life and in his suffering. The Church gives special honor to those who bear the stigmata, the physical signs of Jesus' Passion. But the truth is that we are all stigmatists; we all bear the wounds of Christ, not by any merit of ours, but by God's pure gift. Does it make sense for a stigmatist to ask that the wounds of Christ be removed? If we suffer only because we refuse to love, then we gain nothing. But to share in the wounds of Christ is a great honor.

So, let us rejoice in our suffering. Whatever may be our natural human reactions to the suffering we encounter, we need to remember that these crosses and the wounds they inflict on us are our greatest dignity. Let us smile with joy in the midst of our afflictions. Our wounds are the seeds of our resurrection. If we are insulted or cursed because of Christ, we are blessed because the Spirit of the Lord rests upon us. Let us not be ashamed to bear a portion of the one whose love for us was so great that he gave of himself in suffering, even unto death on a Cross.

Day 31 | Surrendering to the Wounds of the Cross

If one asks him, "What are these wounds on your back?" he will say, "The wounds I received in the house of my friends."

—Zechariah 13:6

The words "I thirst"—do they echo in our souls? . . . especially when humiliation and suffering come? They have to come. What is my first thought? I will pick the roses. The sharper the thorns, the sweeter shall be my song . . . to satiate the thirst of Jesus by total surrender— complete, without counting the cost.

—Mother Teresa (Instructions, 1980)

As Jesus went to Calvary, he was inwardly assenting to the will of the Father, embracing the Cross that had been laid upon him on behalf of his friends. He submitted to the wickedness of men to win grace and strength for us, so that we might grow in the desire to surrender to the goodness of the Father.

What is Jesus teaching us by the wounds he received? Those wounds are our thirst for him, our union with him. Surrendering to the goodness of the Father, like Jesus did on the road to Calvary, is our only path to holiness. Satan knows this, and he fears our surrender to God above everything else, above every other virtue or good work. He will fight it with unceasing energy and with the most logical and holy arguments. Like Jesus, we need to resist him, and say, "Get behind me, Satan! I wish to think as the Father does, and not as man does" (see Mk 8:33).

In all that befell him, Jesus remained focused on the Person of the Father. He did not allow himself to get lost in the immediate event, in the specific injustice, in this or that person, in the means or the instruments of his suffering. At every moment of his Passion, Jesus was standing face to face with his Father.

Just as this was the key for Jesus in going to the Cross, so it is for us. We need to view our surrender as Jesus did. True surrender always leads to an encounter with the Father in Jesus. To embrace the wood of the Cross is to embrace the Crucified One fastened there. Very often our failure to rightly surrender to the Cross is due to the fact that we mistake the object of our surrender. The object of our surrender is not the suffering we encounter, but the Person of Jesus as he reveals the Father. If we look at the instrument of suffering alone and fail to see the Father, it is impossible to surrender, and we lose our peace.

What then are these wounds that have afflicted the Lamb of God? They are the signs of his thirst for us, and his surrender for our surrender. Jesus surrenders himself to the wickedness of men to teach us to surrender ourselves to the goodness of the Father. Let us allow our provident Father, who thirsts for us, to bring forth our thirst, to bring forth our surrender through the cup he has chosen, and to give us the vision of his face that we receive when we drink that cup. Let us hear Jesus speaking to us:

"This is my surrender to my Father. This is my thirst for him and for you. And this is his thirst for me. My child, if you ask, what are these wounds I bear? They are your surrender to my Father and your Father. They are your thirst for me and your union with me. Do not reject them, and do not say: they are not just. True, and neither were mine. Your wounds are to be like mine, so that they can become mine. My great pain, as spoken by the prophet, is that I received them in the house of my friends. So shall your wounds be. But be at peace and do not fear; in your wounds, you shall find me. By your wounds, you shall satiate me."

Day 32 | Self-Offering to the Divine Thirst

Now I rejoice in my sufferings for your sake, and in my
flesh I complete what is lacking in Christ's afflictions
for the sake of his body, that is, the Church.

—Colossians 1:24

*O my God, Most Blessed Trinity, Father, Son and Holy Spirit,
I, Mother Teresa, offer myself to you through the Immaculate
Heart of Mary, Mother of the church and my Mother, as a
victim of holocaust to your thirsting love . . .*

—Mother Teresa (Letter, undated)

The very notion of divine thirst includes the all-consuming
desire not only to love, but also to be loved in return in the
same way, with the same totality and ardor, with the same
desire to love and be loved by God. St. John of the Cross has a
famous saying: "*Amor con amor se paga.*" "Love is only repaid by
love." We can apply the same principle here and say, "Thirst
is only repaid by thirst."

The heart of the call to the Missionaries of Charity,
represented in all their chapels with Jesus' cry "I thirst" next to
the crucifix, is a sharing with Jesus of his thirst. It is important
what Jesus asks from us when he says "I thirst." If thirst can
only be repaid by thirst, then the one thing that will satiate
Jesus' thirst for us is our own thirst for him in return. In the
words of St. Augustine, "*Deus sitit sitiri*"—"God thirsts to be

thirsted for." But what better testimony to this truth can we
have than the words of Jesus himself: "If any one thirst, let
him come to me and drink" (Jn 7:37).

God's thirst for us came in the form of a gift: the total
outpouring of his Son and Spirit into our poverty. Our thirst
for him requires a similar self-gift, a similar "outpouring" in
oblation. (The term *oblation* derives from the Latin word for
the act of "pouring out.") As Jesus made his total oblation by
emptying himself to prove his thirst for us, so we pour ourselves
out in our response of thirst for him. Such an oblation is our
commitment to satiate his thirst; it is our personal consecration
to the thirst of his Sacred Heart. The Oblation to Divine
Thirst is an expression of love for love, of gift for gift, of thirst
for thirst. It involves the total gift of self in all circumstances
in order to experience, to live, to serve, and to proclaim the
mystery of God's thirst.

The elements of this oblation are simple:

First: We have the intention of giving all to satiate Jesus'
thirst, wholeheartedly, holding nothing back, and without
counting the cost. Nothing is excluded. Our prayer, our
sacrifices, our service, and our suffering are offered for this
purpose, which is the goal of our lives and the object of all our
energies and desires. All for his thirst and only for his thirst.

Second: We will make a personal covenant with the Lord:
"You will be mine, and I will be yours; without reserve, and
forever." We will willingly take on all his concerns in satiating
and making known his thirst, and we will abandon all our
concerns into his hands. In complete trust that Jesus will be
faithful to his part of the covenant by caring for us, we will
surrender all our concerns to him. We are confident that

he will concern himself with all our affairs, temporal and spiritual, to the extent that we concern ourselves with his. We know that we will be satiated to the extent that we abandon all other worries and concerns to satiate only him in whatever way of life or service he has given us.

Third: We will offer ourselves as vessels and channels for God's thirsting love to a waiting world, to give his thirst in our charity, intercede for it by our prayer and suffering, and proclaim it in our words and example. We desire to be apostles of Jesus' thirst, twenty-four hours a day, in season and out of season, whatever it may cost us.

Prayer of Oblation to the Divine Thirst

I (n . . .) offer myself in oblation, wholly and forever, to satiate and proclaim the infinite thirst of the Father, Son, and Holy Spirit for love and souls revealed in Jesus' great cry of thirst from the Cross. Henceforth, I take this as the sole purpose of my life and the sole intention of all my acts, abandoning all else into your hands, O Lord, and giving you the most complete freedom over me and all that concerns me, that I may quench your thirst in whatever you may choose in your providence. I make this Oblation through the Immaculate Heart of Mary, Cause of Our Joy, and into her hands I entrust my desire to satiate her Son in humility, faithfulness, and generosity.

VI.
Jesus, the Incarnation of God's Thirst

Day 33 | The Mystery of the Cross

You call me Teacher and Lord; and you are right, for so I am. If I then, your Lord and Teacher, have washed your feet, you also ought to wash one another's feet.

—John 13:13–14

Do you feel the thirst of Jesus? Do you hear his voice? . . . I will satiate his thirst. Who are the poorest of the poor? Nobody but you and me! We are the poorest of the poor. Begin first with me, then the community, step by step. . . . Be sincere, humble with Jesus.

—Mother Teresa (Instructions, 1994)

The Passion of Christ—his betrayal by Judas, his capture by his enemies, his trial, his scourging, the Via Dolorosa, and finally his Crucifixion—was Jesus' moment of glory, when he was expressing the Father's thirst for humanity in all its depth and was winning for his disciples their union with the Father. For us, as for his first disciples, there is a deep mystery here, the mystery of the Cross, the instrument of death that mysteriously becomes the tree of life.

At the Last Supper, Jesus prepares his disciples for the mystery of the Cross. Before he gives the gift of his Body and Blood in the Eucharist and on Calvary, he wants to draw them into the spirit of this grace and teach them how to live this gift. The commandment of charity and the invitation to suffer, to follow him to Calvary, are the fruits and proof that the disciples are living the gift, thirsting for him, and genuinely satiating his thirst for them and for others.

Before Jesus breaks the bread in the first Eucharist and mounts the wood of the Cross of Calvary, he wants the disciples to be clear about the meaning behind what he is going to do and suffer. So he takes a towel and water (a symbol of healing and of the Holy Spirit), and he washes their feet. He does the work of the lowliest slave in a Jewish household. Let us consider this for a moment: the Master of the universe washing the feet of the Twelve Apostles. He does this first of all to cleanse them, and secondly to teach them that he has not come to be served but to serve, to give his life as a ransom. He also shows them that the spilling of his blood would be their healing and cleansing.

All eyes are on Jesus at this moment. Many thoughts are passing through the minds of the disciples. What a tremendous paradox: he, the Master, doing the work of a slave! He who is Lord and King has come to serve! Imagine this happening to you—Jesus himself washing your feet. The disciples are shocked; yet at the same time they are beginning to understand just how much Jesus loves them. Even so, this lowly and loving act is only the beginning of the expression of Jesus' charity.

Having performed this amazing service for his disciples, Jesus then tells them that they are to do the same for one another. Jesus wishes to continue, through our hands, the healing and the cleansing of a broken, sullied world. Jesus glorifies the Father in us to the extent that we continue to live this mystery of service and of suffering and accept his plan of self-gift. Let us not answer as Peter did: "You shall never wash my feet!" (Jn 13:8). If we say "no" to that washing, what a waste it will be. Only if he first washes us can he then wash others through us. If we refuse to be healed and cleansed ourselves, we will not be a channel of his healing and cleansing to our brothers and sisters. If we allow him to fill and satiate us, then he can satiate others through us. By our Baptism, he is in us; and because he is in us, he can bless, heal, wash, serve, and satiate others through us.

In the Eucharist, the mystery of the Church is revealed: many grains, one bread; many grapes, one wine. As the bread is one, the body is to be one. If we want our Eucharist to be real, we need to be ready to wash one another's feet, whether of wounds, poverty, or misery.

We are called to reveal both the thirsting and the satiating of Jesus. This mutual washing reflects the life of mutual self-giving of the Trinity. My weakness exists for another's gifts, and my gift exists for another's weakness. Let each of us use the gifts we have been given so that in everything God may be glorified through Jesus Christ.

Day 34 | The Agony of Gethsemane

Then Jesus went with them to a place called Gethsemane, and he said to his disciples, "Sit here, while I go over there and pray." And taking with him Peter and the two sons of Zebedee, he began to be sorrowful and troubled. Then he said to them, "My soul is very sorrowful, even to death; remain here, and watch with me."

—Matthew 26:36–38

That terrible longing keeps growing—& I feel as if something will break in me one day—and then that darkness, that loneliness, that feeling of terrible aloneness. Heaven from every side is closed ... and yet—I long for God. I long to love Him with every drop of life in me—and I want to love Him with a deep personal love.

—Mother Teresa[*]

The suffering that Jesus endures in the Garden of Gethsemane is at the core of the Passion. But before the actual events take place, Jesus gives his "yes" to the Father. He will not be dragged against his will through everything that is about to occur. His "yes" contains all that those events will mean. He sees everything that is about to be heaped upon him—all our sin and rejection—all it will cost him, and in his thirsting love, he still says "yes."

---

[*] Mother Teresa, *Come Be My Light*. Fr. Brian Kolodiejchuk, M.C., editor. (New York: Doubleday), 2007, 202–203.

Agony here refers to the final struggle with the violent forces of evil, a direct battle against all of Hell's power: suffering, pain, fear, horror, and death. It takes great humility to allow others to see us in our moments of weakness. Yet Jesus did so. He wanted witnesses to this ineffable struggle, so he chose the same three Apostles who had seen his glory at the Transfiguration. Through this act of humility he gained infinite glory by an almost infinite agony. At the same time, he obtained graces for us in our temptations and struggles and left us an example of how to face them.

In the Garden of Gethsemane, Jesus was afflicted by three sentiments: he faced sadness unto death; he experienced rejection and disgust; and he knew horror and fear. He asked his disciples to watch and pray with him, but they were overcome with sleep. We will want to accompany him in his agony, to stay awake so that we can watch and pray with him.

Jesus was sad for Judas, whom he loved and wanted to save, but whom he knew would be lost. He was sad for all the lost souls whom he had thirsted for, even to the end of time. He was sad for Peter, so good, yet so inconstant, overly sure of himself and shallow in his love. He was sad for all those he would choose as his special disciples who would fall into the slumber of spiritual tepidity, whose spirit was willing but whose flesh was weak. He was sad for all the Apostles, knowing that they would abandon him and run away at the time of his need. He was sad for his beloved Israel, for those chosen by his Father but who had rejected their Messiah. He was sad for Jerusalem, the holy city, soon to be shattered and destroyed.

Jesus had taken upon himself all the sins of a fallen race. He mystically embraced the experience of being rejected and scorned, cast off and accursed. He was shown by Satan all that had been lost: all those who would reject the Father's love, all the horror and pain of slavery to sin. He encountered not only the suffering he would soon endure, but the sufferings of the whole human race. He heard the laughter and mockery of the devil, who thought this was his moment of triumph, and who tempted him with the supposed worthlessness of his sacrifice.

The greatest darkness that Jesus encountered was the weight of an almost limitless guilt. Though innocent himself, he took on himself the guilt of all. What this meant we can hardly imagine. We know the pain of guilt, even over one serious sin. What must it have been to have the whole burden of guilt and shame carried upon his shoulders? "For our sake he made him to be sin who knew no sin, so that in him we might become the righteousness of God" (2 Cor 5:21).

Then, as now, Jesus thirsts for our love. Let us stay awake, watching and praying with him, and, like the angel sent from Heaven, console him in his anguish. By this means we can enter his thirst and so share his life.

Day 35 | Peter and Judas

As it is, I rejoice, not because you were grieved,
but because you were grieved into repenting;
for you felt a godly grief, so that you suffered no loss
through us. For godly grief produces a repentance
that leads to salvation and brings no regret,
but worldly grief produces death.

—2 Corinthians 7:9–10

*When I look at "I thirst," there was so much pain, so much
of his Precious Blood lost through the scourging and
crowning with thorns. Let us see our sins in that Precious
Body, in every drop of his blood. I was present . . . my sins
were present there. It is not sentimental. Don't close your
eyes; look, find my sins there, my uncharitableness.*

—Mother Teresa (Instructions, 1984)

Peter and Judas: two men, two disciples, caught up in the events surrounding the Passion of Jesus. Let us briefly compare these two souls. There are some surprising similarities between them.

- Both were chosen by Christ to be Apostles.
- Both knew Jesus and shared his life during his public ministry.
- Both had heard Jesus' teaching and had seen his miracles.

- Both had preached the Gospel under Jesus' direction and had worked miracles themselves.

- Both were warned of their coming fall into sin at the Last Supper.

- Both were warned that Satan would seek to sift them like wheat.

- Both grievously failed Jesus.

- Both were personally invited to repentance.

- Both felt tremendous remorse for what they had done.

Yet for all the similarities, there are very important differences between the two men, especially in the way they responded to their failure. From the first, Peter's focus was on Jesus; his sorrow was over the pain he had given to his Master. Judas's focus was on himself; his sorrow was over the monstrous sin he had committed and over his own horrible deed. What a terrible thing he had done! How could he have fallen so low?

When we regret our sins because we hate our shame, when we indulge in self-condemnation, when we focus on what great sinners we are and on how foolish we have been, when we ask how we could possibly have done this, when, in short, we become preoccupied with the self, all of this engenders in us the sadness of pride, an unholy sadness that can lead to despair and death, as it did for Judas.

Because Peter's sadness and remorse was focused on the one he had pained, his sorrow led him back to Jesus and to a new strength fortified by a newer and deeper humility and love. His was a sadness that led to joy. The great tragedy of Judas is that he could have done what Peter had done. Had he changed the focus of his soul from himself to Jesus, he could have become a great saint even with his faults and his fall.

When we draw close to the Lord in prayer and honesty, he often shows us our poverty, our weaknesses, and our mistakes, not to condemn us, but to address what is corrupt in us and to heal it. As with Peter, our failures are meant to lead us back to the Lord. If our remorse is like that of Peter, it will bear fruit and lead to joy. In his deep thirst for us, Christ uses everything—even our sins, surprising as that is—to bring us to himself. If we humbly let go of our sins, and give them to Jesus, if we think of the harm and the pain they have caused him rather than the shame and self-contempt they have caused us, we will allow Jesus to turn that pain into healing. So, by all means let us repent; let us be sorry for our sins. But let us keep our eyes fixed, not on our sins and on ourselves, but on Christ our Savior.

Day 36 | Jesus and Pilate

Pilate said to him, "So you are a king?" Jesus answered, "You say that I am a king. For this I was born, and for this I have come into the world, to bear witness to the truth. Every one who is of the truth hears my voice." Pilate said to him, "What is truth?"

—John 18:37–38

The mysteries of Jesus that Holy Mother Church helps us to relive during Holy Week and Easter must be very specially dear to every Missionary of Charity, for it is the mystery of the distressing disguise of Jesus, crucified by sin and for sin. It is this mystery that most fully reveals the depth of God's thirst to draw us back to his love.

—Mother Teresa (Instructions, 1996)

The Sanhedrin, the Council of Jewish elders, did not want Jesus to die on their hands, thus making him into a martyr. They did not want to use religious reasons as their excuse for killing him because then he would seem to be dying a prophet's death, which would appear noble in the eyes of the people. They wanted him to be viewed as a common criminal, acknowledged as such and therefore put to death by Rome, the symbol of universal, impartial justice. So they took him to Pontius Pilate, the Roman Procurator. Pilate could see something of the pride and envy that was motivating their accusations. Pilate was an ex-general, proud, ambitious, and no lover of the Jews, but he had an innate sense of fairness. He intended to release Jesus since he could find no crime committed by him, but at the same time he felt the need to protect himself.

When Pilate questioned Jesus about whether he was king of the Jews as his accusers had claimed, Jesus appealed to Pilate's integrity. He spoke to him of truth and invited him to open his heart. But Pilate refused the grace, fearing that the price was too high. He vacillated; he was indecisive; he wanted to find a substitute good. Avoiding the claims of truth, he excused his conscience by escaping into relativity. "What is truth," he said to Jesus, as if to say: "God's will? Who knows? God has not given me any concrete proof, so I will do what I want, where I want, when I want, and how I want. My version of truth is all that matters."

We can see in this encounter the concern Jesus had for Pilate's salvation despite the great pain the Roman was about to inflict upon him. Jesus was expressing the Father's forgiving, thirsting love for Pilate. He was constant in self-forgetfulness in order to satiate the Father's thirst for souls, despite all the humiliations involved.

Having refused to face the truth in its fullness, Pilate tried to find a middle way. He said to Jesus, in effect: "I won't be your disciple; but I don't want to put you to death." He tried to appease the crowd, first by having Jesus scourged, and then attempting to have him released. But neither tactic worked. His compromises with grace led him where he did not want to go, to responsibility for Jesus' Death. Finally he abdicated his responsibility to choose what was right. He symbolically but uselessly washed his hands and delivered Jesus up to be crucified.

Pilate's fate is a lesson in the danger of indecisiveness in the face of the call of Christ. No doubt there were good reasons for his vacillating; there are always good reasons for dodging God's word. But truth has an authority of its own, and we need to respond to the promptings and challenges of grace, lest we too find ourselves led down roads that we did not want to travel.

Day 37 | "I Thirst"

After this Jesus, knowing that all was now finished, said (to fulfil the Scripture), "I thirst." A bowl of vinegar stood there; so they put a sponge full of the vinegar on hyssop and held it to his mouth.

—John 19:28–29

From the cross Jesus cries out "I thirst." His thirst was for souls even as he hung there dying, alone, despised. Who will bring those souls to him to satiate that thirst of the infinite God dying of love? Can you and I continue to stand by, a mere spectator? Or pass by and do nothing?

—Mother Teresa (Address, 1986)

This is the supreme moment, when Jesus, in the name of the Father, speaks of God's infinite thirst for each one of us. It is important that we hear his words and allow them to enter and penetrate our hearts, shedding their light on every detail of our lives such that they come to live within us. The answers to all our questions are ultimately to be found in the light of these words and through the lens of this moment. Any darkness that may trouble us, whether within us or around us, will find its light here—a light and a fire that has the potential to set everything ablaze. It does not matter who we are or what we have been; this fire consumes and transforms everything into itself. It touches on a mystery too deep and too sacred to approach alone. That is why Our Lady is present at the

Cross as Jesus speaks these words to us. Like John, we need to take Our Lady's hand in order to hear and respond to Jesus as he speaks of the Trinity's thirst for us, and to understand what is to be our thirst in return. Our Lady will aid us by her presence, her prayer, and her example.

Let us consider the Blessed Mother at the Cross. This is Our Lady of Sorrows, our suffering mother following her Son to Calvary. She witnesses his sufferings and suffers unspeakable pain, and Jesus experiences the pain of seeing his beloved mother suffer for his sake. In this mystery she is more mother to us than ever. Jesus says to John, just at this moment: "Behold, your Mother." As we place ourselves in Mary's heart and see with her eyes, we will perceive the depth of his thirsting love for us—even as we are, even as you were, at our worst. The pain of Jesus becomes his word of Revelation, his own blood that speaks so eloquently.

Let us consider, even to the point of tasting something of his pain of body and spirit, that Jesus could have ended his suffering at any moment had he so decided. He could have called upon the Father for legions of angels and thereby avoided this whole anguishing trial. But he did not. He willingly surrendered himself to man's wickedness so that we might learn to surrender ourselves to God's goodness. Our place is to make ourselves one with Jesus as he gives himself to the Father and to unite our offering, whatever suffering we are enduring, to his.

As we stand beneath the Cross with Our Lady, we come to realize that when we concentrate on Jesus' Passion and not our own, our pain can become his, and his strength can become ours. Christ and his Cross, and the words he spoke from the Cross, are our only (and yet our constant) source of strength.

Let us then hear Jesus say to each one of us, "I thirst!" with his eyes fixed on us. In that gaze we can find the eternal thirst of the Father for us. Here at the foot of the Cross we can remain, not to try and feel much, not even to try to console, but simply to be present and allow Jesus to take us deeper into his thirst for us.

Day 38 | Holy Saturday

For Christ also died for sins once for all, the righteous for the unrighteous, that he might bring us to God, being put to death in the flesh but made alive in the spirit; in which he went and preached to the spirits in prison, who formerly did not obey.

—1 Peter 3:18–20

We are meant to satiate the thirst of Jesus, and this thirst was revealed to us from the Cross. We cannot know or satiate the thirst of Jesus if we do not know, love, and live the Cross of Jesus. We must be united with Jesus in our suffering, with our hearts full of love for the Father and love for souls as his was.

—*Mother Teresa (Letter, 1996)*

Holy Saturday, the time when Christ is in the tomb, can give us a unique insight into the thirst of Jesus. Let us imaginatively accompany Our Lady as she goes through this quiet period of the Passion. The Sabbath had already begun late on Friday as Our Lady walked back to the Upper Room from the events of the day. How crushing a day it had been for her. What she had seen and experienced would be forever burned into her memory. She continued to have faith in God, but she was now in the grip of pain and solitude.

As she enters the Upper Room, she finds Peter at the table weeping over his denial of Jesus. Our Lady comes to him, and, in the name of Jesus, gives his initial intimation of absolution, the first fruits of Jesus' Crucifixion and Death. "Peter, do you know what he said before he died? 'Father forgive them.' He has already forgiven you, Peter." The redeemed Church, washed clean in the blood of Christ, then began to beat in the heart of Peter. The sinful but forgiven Church was being born that night through Mary's ministry. She fixes a meal for the Apostles and has them sit down at table, remembering what Jesus said and did. Later, as they go dragging off to sleep one by one, she blows out the lamp.

Our Lady awakens to the emptiness of Saturday morning. There is no voice of Jesus. She passes the Sabbath day without him. How distant Heaven then seems to her. Like Jesus on the Cross, her heart is living in the darkness of faith: "My God, why have you abandoned me?" She makes breakfast for the disciples, and again helps them to center their minds away from themselves and toward Jesus and what he had done for each of them. Their community is strengthened, as Our Lady performs her special role, building up the Church.

At one point during the day, John takes Peter to Calvary. He shows Peter the place where Jesus was nailed and where the Cross stood. As he describes the scene, he shows him the blood on the ground, the great cracks in the earth from the moment when Jesus died. He tells Peter of the great love he had seen in Jesus' eyes as he spoke those heartrending words: "I thirst."

Later in the evening, Our Lady is alone in the Upper Room and praying in silence, turning over in her heart all the events of the past week, and understanding the mystery of redemption all the more deeply for having seen and lived it. She thinks about all the good that will come. This very room will be the beginning of the Church, the fount of mankind's hope. She shares the gift of hope first of all with the eleven

Apostles who are so shaken and badly in need of it. Many of the women of Jesus' company had come throughout the day to console Mary in her loss, but it was she who strengthened and consoled them. From the beginning, she was Our Lady of Hope.

In the Temple all is chaos and confusion. The veil is still torn; the sacrifices have stopped. There is an atmosphere of suppressed guilt, in all the hasty meetings, the arguments, divisions, the fearful talk of the prophecy of the Resurrection. The only thing the authorities can agree on is that this so-called Resurrection must never happen. So envoys are sent to Pilate, and he sets a seal on the tomb and guards to watch it. These very guards will be the first to witness and tell of Jesus' rising. But now all is yet darkness and desolation.

And in his dark dominion, Satan trembles, and with him all his hosts, as the full import of the Death of Jesus begins to take effect.

VII.
Satiated Thirst

Day 39 | Easter Serenity

Now on the first day of the week, Mary Magdalene came to the tomb early, while it was still dark, and saw that the stone had been taken away from the tomb.

—John 20:1

Look at Mary Magdalene; she was so in love with Jesus. She went early in the morning to see him....Are we like that at holy Mass, prayer? Do we have that eagerness and longing to be with him and run to him?

—Mother Teresa (Instructions, 1994)

Easter is a time of serenity. The special serenity of this day is the fruit not only of Good Friday, but also of Holy Saturday, of Jesus' "descending into hell" as the Creed puts it. Jesus has descended deeply into the nether world of our souls. He has entered those areas of brokenness and darkness within us and filled them with his life and light. He has then raised us up and given us a new hope built on Easter faith. The resurrected Jesus can only be grasped by faith; he comes and goes as he chooses, when he chooses, where he chooses. We cannot cling to him any longer through our senses, but only in the Spirit and in truth through faith. Because of Jesus' great thirst for us he does not restrict himself to coming only in certain times or ways. Thanks to the victory of the Resurrection, he, the second Adam, has become a life-giving spirit (see 1 Cor 15:45). He is now free to express his thirst at all times and places, to wrap himself in the veil of every event, each circumstance, and every distressing disguise. Thanks to the Resurrection, we need not run to the tomb like the Magdalene in the anxious hope of finding him, or in fear that someone may have stolen him from us. He promised us that he would be with us always.

That is why Easter joy is peaceful. For Jesus is now present no longer just in Galilee or on Golgotha, but in all things. From Easter day forward, all the winding halls of time resound: "I thirst!" We are witnesses of the Resurrection of Christ, not because we were physically in Jerusalem, but because we have eaten and drunk with him. Since his Resurrection, Jesus has shared his risen life with us. We are those chosen ones who have known the power of his Resurrection. We have been immersed into the living waters, baptized into Christ's Death and Resurrection. It is our call to continue to share our communion with the Risen Lord, drinking in his presence, his satiating, his healing, and the power of his Resurrection. As witnesses of the Resurrection, we are called not only to talk about the thirst of God, but also to know the power of the Spirit, and to taste the thirst of the Father "poured into our hearts" (Rom 5:5).

On our altars, we are present not only to Calvary but also to the Resurrection: to the risen, glorified Christ, who praises the Father and intercedes for us. Though we cannot now see him, behind this veil the Lamb stands victorious and glorious before the Father. The humility, the poverty, and the hiddenness of the Eucharist veils our glorious Lord.

Let us then be who we are called to be, and where we are called to be, at the Father's right hand by virtue of Jesus' Resurrection and our Baptism into him. The deepest part of us is already risen with the Lord—we are already seated at the right hand of the Father with him. We are now waiting for the full effect of the Spirit in us. But we are risen in Christ; it is just a matter of time. So let our thoughts be in Heaven, rather than fixed on a passing earth. As Paul writes, "You have died, and your life is hidden with Christ in God" (Col 3:3).

We are the witnesses of this invisible reality, hidden under the veil of poverty, failure, and weakness. We do not need to wait for our own bodily resurrection. A life hidden with Christ in the Father as he stands in prayer, satiation, and intercession is our call, our special dignity, our very life.

Day 40 | The Gift of the Holy Spirit

**All who are led by the Spirit of God are sons
of God. For you did not receive the spirit of slavery
to fall back into fear, but you have received the
spirit of sonship. When we cry, "Abba! Father!"
it is the Spirit himself bearing witness with our
spirit that we are children of God.**

—Romans 8:14–16

*To show forth the luminous face of Jesus
radiant with purity—radiant!*

—Mother Teresa (Instructions, 1981)

Throughout his time on earth, Jesus was preparing the people of Israel, and in a special way his own disciples, for his "hour" of glory on Calvary—the revelation of the Father as thirsting love. Yet those most sacred words, "I thirst," were not an end in themselves; they were meant to prepare us for the great gift, the communication of God's thirsting love in the outpouring of the Holy Spirit. The revelation of Jesus' thirst on Calvary prepared the way for the communication of Jesus' thirst on the day of Pentecost.

The Holy Spirit is himself the thirst of the Father and Son—he is the gift of love by which they eternally and infinitely surrender themselves to each other. If this Spirit of love is capable of satiating the infinite thirst of the Almighty, can this gift not satiate the thirst of our hearts and of all the world? And will this omnipotent Spirit not be able to purify and divinize my own human thirst for God so as to satiate him as he would wish? Everything depends on the gift of the Holy Spirit—both the satiating of God and the satiating of man.

Without the Holy Spirit, the Trinity collapses in disunity. Without the Holy Spirit, the Gospel is a dead letter, the Church is only an organization, the words of Jesus on the Cross are merely history, the Resurrection has no connection with us, the sacraments are empty rituals, Jesus is a distant memory, the Missionaries of Charity are merely a group of social workers, and the poor are nothing other than hopeless victims in a hopeless world.

But with the Holy Spirit all is transformed. The Gospel then becomes the living Word of God; the Church is the very Body of Christ; Jesus' words on the Cross, "I thirst," become an invitation to every person; the Resurrection is our own victory over sin and death; the sacraments are vessels of eternal life; Jesus is closer to us than we are to ourselves; the MCs are the voice of his thirst in the world and a channel of his satiation; and the poor are the very face of Christ. And, above all, the thirsting love of God is poured into every human heart so that each person can be satiated by God and can satiate him in return. The prophetic symbolism of the Feast of Tabernacles has now been fulfilled: the crucified and glorified Son of God has revealed the thirst of the Father and has poured out upon the parched desert of our world the living waters of the Holy Spirit. Our own desert begins to bloom, as the Holy Spirit satiates our thirst and makes us capable of loving so as to satiate the thirst of God.

If the Holy Spirit is really the "living waters" that Jesus promised, why did he descend as tongues of fire? Throughout the Scriptures, the Holy Spirit is likened to both fire and water. How does this fit with Jesus' cry of thirst from the Cross? Let us consider this double symbolism of fire and water.

As to fire, God's thirst to love and be loved is indeed a *"devouring fire"* (Dt 4:24). It is something ardent, dynamic, burning, and transforming. Anyone who has experienced thirst knows that it is indeed a kind of fire. The Holy Spirit, the thirsting love of Father and Son, is well portrayed as he came on Pentecost as the living fire of God's love. God's thirst to love and be loved is the consuming fire of the Holy Spirit.

As to water, as we saw earlier, thirst can only be repaid by thirst, or, in St. Augustine's words, "God thirsts to be thirsted for." The fire of our thirst quenches the fire of God's thirst. And the fire of God's thirst—the Holy Spirit—quenches the fire of our thirst, for nothing else will ever satisfy us.

The Holy Spirit is thus like a fire to the one who loves (be it God or man), and like living waters to the one who is receiving love. We experience the Holy Spirit as both: as a fire inflaming our hearts with thirst for God, and as living water when we experience God's thirst for us. Through this double symbolism we are shown once again that God thirsts for our thirst, and that his thirst will overflow and satiate the whole world.

Epilogue | Keeping Our Eyes on the Reward

But, as it is written, "What no eye has seen, nor ear heard, nor the heart of man conceived, what God has prepared for those who love him," God has revealed to us through the Spirit. For the Spirit searches everything, even the depths of God.

—1 Corinthians 2:9–10

The more we understand this thirst of Jesus, the more united and the closer we come to Jesus because it is the tremendous thirst of Jesus' heart. . . . Just think, God is thirsting for you and me to come forward to satiate his thirst. Just think of that!

—Mother Teresa (Instructions, 1997)

To experience the thirst of God for us during our earthly pilgrimage is already to find living waters welling up within us, bringing us a peace and a sense of fulfillment that the world cannot give. Yet, as Jesus tells us, the living waters of his thirst are the mysterious, hidden beginnings of eternal life, welling up to eternal life. The first stirrings of the Spirit of love within us do indeed satiate us; yet as long as this earthly life lasts, we long for more, for complete fulfillment where Christ sits at the right hand of God.

Our full and lasting satiation will be realized only in the kingdom. Our taste of it here below makes us yearn for the full gift, and thirst for Heaven. Was this yearning not one of the most remarkable characteristics of the early Christians, for whom the memory of Jesus was still so fresh and alive? Their proximity to Jesus produced their thirst for Heaven—a sign of having truly met Jesus' thirst. If we find that we do not experience the same yearning, it means the Lord is calling us to a deeper and richer encounter with his thirst.

The yearning we are speaking of is not simply a feeling, but instead a deep desire of the will, meant to be our habitual state after discovering, or rediscovering, God's thirsting love for us in Christ. We can see it at work in Paul. After his experience of meeting Jesus on the road to Damascus, he was constantly torn between his desire to satiate Jesus in fruitful labor among his brothers, and his desire to be satiated by him in glory, *to depart and be with Christ, for that is far better*. The true Christian knows the same tension, and echoes Paul when he says: "Which I shall choose I cannot tell. I am hard pressed between the two" (Phil 1:22–23).

"What no eye has seen nor ear heard . . ." We can have no human idea of the glory of heaven, but the Spirit, the living water of God's love, has already begun to reveal it to us by giving us to drink of the Lord's thirst. John tells us that "we shall be like him"—that we shall become a pure thirsting love for God—because "we shall see him as he is" (1 Jn 3:2). Even now, the encounter of Jesus' thirst awakens and brings forth our own thirst for him. We know what love and desire the rare touches of grace can produce in our spirits even on this side of the veil. We can only imagine the total, joyful, ecstatic, ceaseless pouring forth of self in love and union that awaits us with the full unveiled experience of God's infinite thirst for us.

As we bring to a close our meditations on God's thirst, let us remember Jesus' words, that "the measure you give will be the measure you get" (Mt 7:2). The degree of my thirst for Jesus on earth will be the degree of my satiation in glory. The eternal encounter with the full force of Jesus' thirst will not be a static experience; instead it will be an eternal, ever deeper "voyage" into the divine thirst. This mystery is already at work within us. Our spiritual resurrection and ascension in Baptism is the seed of our full resurrection and ascension in the coming kingdom. The living waters are already poured into our hearts, and the experience of Jesus' thirst will continue to grow, welling up within us to eternal life.

What's the big deal about being Catholic? ▶